I Had My Baby!

A Pediatrician's

Essential Guide

to the First 6 Months

Robert Lindeman, MD, PhD

Lesson Ladder
Success within reach!

www.lessonladder.com
25 First Street, Cambridge, MA 02141

XAMonline, Inc., Cambridge, MA 02141

To obtain permission(s) to use the material from this work for any purpose, including workshops or seminars, please submit a written request to:

Lesson Ladder: an imprint of XAMonline, Inc.
25 First Street, Suite 106, Cambridge, MA 02141

Toll Free: 1-800-301-4647
Fax: 1-617-583-5552
Email: customerservice@lessonladder.com
Web: www.lessonladder.com

Text: Robert Lindeman, MD, PhD

Illustrations: Rachel Enos and Angela Montoya
Cover photos: BananaStock/80403082/Thinkstock; Digital Vision/dv1171053/Thinkstock
Book Design: iiCREATIVE
Production: nSight, Inc.

Library of Congress Catalog Card Number: (pending)
Lindeman, Robert, MD, PhD
I Had My Baby! A Pediatrician's Essential Guide to the First 6 Months   244 pp., ill

1. Title
2. Infants (newborn) – care – popular works
3. Infants (newborn) – health and hygiene – popular works
4. Infant care – handbooks
5. Child development – popular works
6. Child rearing – popular works

RJ61 L563 2012   649.122 L641 2012
ISBN: 978-0-9848657-4-1

Dedication

To Noah and Evan
On whom all this stuff was field-tested

Acknowledgements

In this, my first attempt to write a book, I owe several debts of gratitude—first, to all my family and friends who have been bugging me for years to write my own book. I have been writing for years for parenting magazines and the web. I've been gratified that so many readers enjoyed my writing, but until now I've resisted the temptation to deliver my opinions and advice in long form. I'm grateful for the opportunity.

I was a son before I was a pediatrician, and my mother, Barbara Lindeman, was my first exemplar and teacher of parenting. My father Philip Lindeman (of blessed memory) was an attorney who wrote beautifully. I hope he would be proud of the writing in these pages.

I acknowledge my wife, Deborah Lindeman, from whom I learned as much about parenting as she learned pediatrics from me. Deborah was a developmental editor during life-before-kids. She read several of the early chapters and provided useful and helpful advice. Deborah was a natural editor for my text because she knew most of it by heart already: When our boys were young, we often received phone calls from friends with babies, looking for some advice from the doctor. Deborah always listened to their question, and then, having heard me counsel parents on the phone countless times, she responded, "OK, here's what he's going to say..."

I'm indebted also to Jessica Ferreira, pediatric nurse practitioner, a colleague, and a friend, who read a rough draft of this book and provided many helpful suggestions.

To Beth Kaufman at Lesson Ladder, who approached me in early 2012 with the opportunity to write a parenting guide, I am eternally grateful. And to Nini Bloch, my developmental editor at Lesson Ladder, to expert reviewer Dr. Christine Traxler, and to the entire crew at that excellent publishing house, for trusting me with the responsibility of writing their first major parenting title.

Finally, it must be said that a book for new parents is by no means a new idea, and many excellent parenting books precede this one. I am humbled to place this volume alongside *Baby and Child Care* by Benjamin Spock, *Baby 411* by my colleague Ari Brown, and the excellent series published by the American Academy of Pediatrics, edited by Stephen Shelov. If on occasion I am able to see farther, it is because I'm standing on the shoulders of giants.

About the Author

Dr. Rob Lindeman has been practicing pediatrics in Massachusetts since 2000. His formal education began at Yale University, where he majored in molecular biochemistry and biophysics. Dr. Lindeman attended medical and graduate school at Columbia University in New York City, earning an MD and a PhD (in physiology). He trained in general pediatrics and pediatric pulmonary medicine at Boston Children's Hospital. In 2005, Dr. Lindeman was appointed Fellow of the American Academy of Pediatrics.

Dr. Lindeman has owned and operated a private pediatrics practice, Natick Pediatrics, since 2002. He and his wife live in Brookline, Massachusetts, with their two boys and a dog.

Contents

Chapter 1: The First Few Days

Chapter 2: Getting to Know Your Baby

Chapter 3: The World Beyond

Chapter 4: Feeding Your Baby

Chapter 5: How to Soothe Your Baby and Calm Crying

Chapter 6: Getting Baby to Sleep

Chapter 7: Growth and Development

Chapter 8: Keeping Baby Healthy

Chapter 9: Vaccinations

Chapter 10: Six Months and Beyond

PREFACE

If you've picked up this book and opened it to this page, chances are you've had a baby or are about to have one. Congratulations!

Why Another Baby Book?

You may ask: Why does the world need another baby book? What does Dr. Rob have to say that's different from what all the other books say?

The major difference between this book and many of the other guides you may have seen has to do with my **philosophy**, which forms the basis for all the advice I give in this book: *I view children as essentially healthy human beings.*

This book will help arm you with the tools you need to be a parent to a baby, *without* feeling the need to Google or call the doctor. My aim is to render my own professional services obsolete. (I doubt I can do anything to make the Internet obsolete!) New parents, even though they've never raised a baby, come to parenthood equipped with more skills and knowledge than they think they have. It's my job to give you the confidence and the conviction that you know more than you think you do.

The Way It Used to Be

Until the 1960s, the philosophy that children are essentially healthy human beings guided most parents, even if they weren't aware they were being so guided. This was certainly the case with my own mother, who gave birth to my oldest sister in 1956. Another sister followed in 1958, and finally my twin sister and I came along in 1964. My mother told me once that she never imagined that she would have anything but perfectly normal children. Indeed, this was the attitude that most mothers held in the 1950s and 1960s, and probably had been the case for generations: Children are basically healthy people to whom stuff happens. At their core, they are healthy.

What Happened?

But something changed between then and now.

By the time I entered training in pediatrics in 1994, the philosophy that had guided my mother's generation had been flipped upside down: Instead of viewing children as essentially healthy people, parents had a tendency to see them as essentially *unhealthy*, or at least as *potentially* unhealthy.

Today, parents bring children to pediatricians' offices, urgent care clinics, and emergency departments at rates far exceeding those of earlier generations. The great irony of all this is that American children are healthier today than they were 50 years ago by any measurement—life expectancy, freedom from disease, safety, and so on. But parents today tend to be much more anxious and worried about their children's health than ever before. Why is this?

Why Do We Worry?

There are many reasons we worry about our children, and they are complex and interrelated. One reason is the human tendency to be skeptical about good news. Our air is cleaner than ever. We can rely on safe supplies of fresh, uncontaminated food and water. And our life expectancy continues to rise, thanks to our prosperity and advances in public health. Yet we seem to worry about our air, food, water, and health more than ever. Likewise with the health of our children: Our children are healthier than ever before in human history, but we tend to worry more than ever about every fever, every cough, and every unexpected behavior.

Another reason we are anxious about our children is that we have evolved (or were created with, if you prefer) a tendency to expect that doom and disaster lurk right around the corner. This tendency served us well when doom and disaster *really did* lurk around the corner, but it serves us badly today when our world is relatively free of these dangers.

Babies Are Healthy and Resilient

I based this book's philosophy on what I believe to be the truth about the health and well-being of children today: They are healthy, they are born healthy, and they are blessed to grow up in a healthy, safe world. To be sure, things happen to kids. They get sick and they get hurt. They always have and they will continue to do so. But children possess an incredible capacity to recover from the most terrible things that nature can throw their way. They certainly are better than adults are at recovering from illnesses.

The "Normal" Trap

The belief that children are essentially healthy affects my view of what's "normal" in kids. Since I was a child, the definition of a "normal" child has become progressively narrower, so that now the number of "abnormal" children is almost greater than the number of "normal" children! My definition of "normal" is broader. I regard the children in my practice as normal first, and then insist that they "prove" to me that they are not normal. I find that this approach saves many healthy children from being subjected to unnecessary testing, diagnoses, and treatments.

This philosophy also tends to steer me away from "medicalizing" normal childhood development and normal variations among children. For example, I don't expect a three-year-old child to sit still and pay attention for very long—yet in today's climate a fidgety kid would find himself scrutinized by adults wary of "attention deficits." Similarly, if a baby is small for her age but her parents are also small and she is growing well, I tend not to subject that baby to a painful (and expensive!) workup for "failure to thrive."

When to Call the Doctor

What this philosophy does not do is cause me to turn a deaf ear to a child's suffering or to ignore signs of a serious illness. If a baby has a fever or is otherwise feeling poorly, I recommend every medication and trick available to make the baby feel better. For this reason I'm pretty quick to recommend medicating a feverish baby with a fever reducer, even if the baby continues to behave and eat normally. If parents have doubts about their baby, I encourage them to call or email me. If the parents' concern does indeed raise the possibility of a problem, I try to aim the family in the most appropriate direction (including toward my office).

Worry Less, Enjoy More

I often describe my job as a process of convincing parents that they are fully able and equipped to take care of a baby, even if they've never done it before. I am there to answer questions, to remove doubts, and to help parents discern the difference between a sick baby that they can care for at home and one that requires my attention. I also describe myself as a filter for all the streams of information flying at them from family, friends, and websites.

I hope this book will convince you that you really can raise your baby on your own and will empower you to find answers when you have doubts. In short, I hope the book will help you worry less about your baby and your parenting skills and allow you to enjoy your baby all the more.

My Approach

When I wrote this book, I had been practicing pediatrics in the community for over 12 years. Tips, tricks, and pearls of wisdom that I've learned from parents and colleagues over the years appear throughout this book.

Prior to becoming a community doctor, I was a so-called academic pediatrician, bringing into practice with me a PhD in physiology and the experience gained in a fellowship in pediatric pulmonary medicine. Training in a hard science made me a much more critical reader of medical literature and a skeptic regarding conclusions drawn from any medical study that hadn't been performed rigorously or hadn't been reproduced in other studies. You will find a fair amount of skepticism in the pages of this book, all of which I hope will help you become more critical readers of the Internet (and even of books like this one!).

I'm also fascinated by the history of medicine. I find that understanding the care of children in the past provides a much-needed perspective on the practice of pediatrics today. You'll find a good deal of historical reference in this book. I hope these sections will help you understand just how fortunate you are to be raising a child in the twenty-first century!

The opinions expressed in this book are only *opinions*, even though I am a professional giver of advice. Nothing in this book should be construed as specific medical advice for *your* child. Always consult your own child's pediatrician. At all times, however, I try to ground my opinions in the best science available. I also try to provide a rational dissection of current debates and hot topics so that parents can make their own decisions. I'm looking to inspire confident and capable parents. Now, go for it!

Look for these bonus sections in every chapter!

A Tip from Dr Rob:

Tips from Dr. Rob
Assuring tips and ideas from an acclaimed pediatrician—it's like having a baby doctor right by your side.

What Now?
From the essential to the simply fascinating, information that will help you put parenting in context and improve your skills.

I Had
My Baby!

- What are the first days in the hospital really like?
- How do you decide between breast and/or bottle?
- How do you prepare for bringing your baby home?
- What are the most important baby-care tips for new parents?

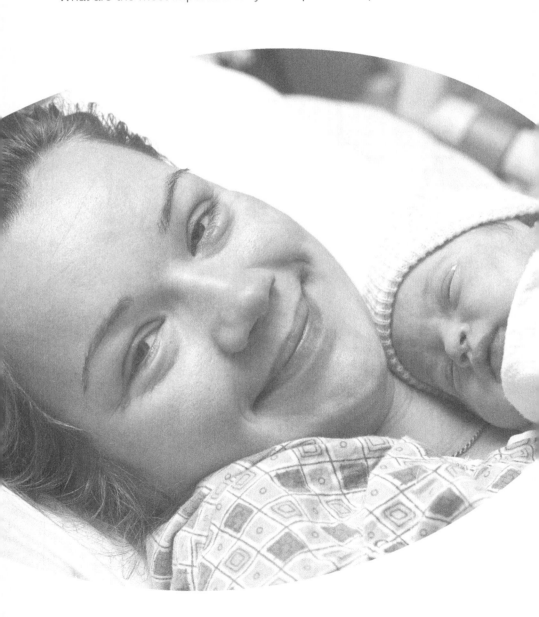

Chapter 1

The First Few Days

Congratulations! You have a new baby! You are about to embark on the toughest, most rewarding job you will ever do: raising a child. There's lots of good news to tell you: Did you know that your child will grow up among the group of healthiest human beings that ever lived? This isn't a wild, outrageous prediction. It's the truth. Every generation since the dawn of time has been healthier and lived longer, on average, than the previous generation. We owe this great success to our prosperity and to improvements in public health, clean food and water, and medicine, in that order. That's something to celebrate. But you have your hands full now. You have a new baby. You can celebrate later.

Every now and then, however, remind yourself of how fortunate you are to be bringing a child into the world *now*. Whatever life brings you from here on out, the odds of your child living a long life without fear of disease and pestilence are much better than they've ever been.

First Days in the Hospital: What to Expect

Chances are you're having your baby in a hospital. Most babies in the developed world are born in hospitals. This is both a good and a bad thing. It's a good thing because hospitals are equipped to handle any bump in the otherwise smooth road to delivering a baby. It's a bad thing because hospitals today are designed to take care of sick people, and pregnant women and babies aren't sick in any meaningful sense of the word. Because hospitals are structured to fit the "sick model," there are lots of things hospitals do that may give you the impression that you and your baby are sick, or at least not entirely well. Don't worry, you're healthier than the hospital makes you think you are. The same goes for your baby: *She* is healthier than the hospital may make you think *she* is!

What happens to my baby right after birth?

From the moment your baby is born doctors and nurses start doing things to her. Before they even place your baby on your stomach or bring her to the warming table, a nurse smears antibiotic goop in your baby's eyes. What's that for?

In the old days, one of the most common causes of blindness was *Gonococcal Ophthalmia*, basically gonorrhea in the eyes. In the twentieth century, researchers discovered that they could protect babies' eyes from gonorrhea by putting an antibiotic ointment in their eyes. Today, we use erythromycin ointment. The American Academy of Pediatrics and the United States Preventive Services Task Force recommends the treatment. As far as we know, there's no downside to using the ointment.

But if you had prenatal care, it might be a good idea to find out if you were checked for gonorrhea. If you were checked, you were negative, and if you haven't contracted gonorrhea between testing and delivery, it's unlikely your baby will get gonorrhea in the eyes. In this case you might consider asking the hospital not to put erythromycin in her eyes. That's because even though there's no real downside to the treatment there's also no particular benefit.

As soon as your baby is born a nurse also gives her a shot of Vitamin K in the leg to prevent a rare but deadly illness called *hemorrhagic disease of the newborn*. For reasons we don't understand babies are born deficient in Vitamin K. It also turns out there's not very much Vitamin K in breast milk. Since Vitamin K is important in blood clotting, without enough Vitamin K babies are at risk of bleeding, even internally. Boys who will be circumcised are especially at risk. Besides the fact that it's a shot, there is no downside to the Vitamin K shot.

What's a new mother to do?

For the precious few days you're still in the hospital, it's a good idea to rest as much as you can, drink more water than you think you need (especially if you're planning to breast-feed), and let the nurses take care of you. Remember: After you go home, even if you've got lots of help, you're still going to have to do a lot more work than you're doing in the hospital. Enjoy the caretaking while it lasts. If you're feeling overwhelmed from all the hard work and exhaustion, it's okay to let the nurses take care of your baby for a while in the nursery to give you the opportunity for some well-deserved sleep.

Who are all these people in my hospital room?

You've just had a baby. You're happy but exhausted. And there is a constant stream of doctors, nurses, food service workers, and cleanup crews parading through your room, often while you're trying to sleep or feed your baby. Why are all these people there, and why do they have to be there?

First of all, it's *your* hospital room and you can expect a considerable degree of privacy. Everybody who comes into your room should knock first and identify himself or herself before barging in. You don't have to let anybody into the room, even if it's the

A Brief History of Maternity Hospitals

Before the eighteenth century babies were born at home. Human beings are unique in that we are the only species on Earth that requires help in delivering our babies. In the past, that help came from an experienced person, almost always a woman, called a *midwife* (from the Old English *mid* [with] -*wif* [wife]). As Europe became increasingly urbanized with large populations of city poor, hospitals were established for the express purpose of serving poor women who could not afford the services of a midwife. The earliest of these hospitals served only married women; a woman needed to produce a marriage certificate to gain admission. Later, so-called lying-in hospitals admitted destitute women of any marital status, including women of means who became pregnant outside of marriage.

From the earliest days of hospital-based maternity, lying-in hospitals were dangerous places. Many women died shortly after childbirth of overwhelming infections called "puerpal fever." The germ theory of disease was 100 years away from discovery, and nobody knew that contagious organisms could be transmitted by touch. The people delivering the babies, most often men, never washed their hands prior to examining a woman in labor. Bacterial infections were passed from bed to bed in this way and took countless lives. A Hungarian obstetrician named Ignaz Semmelweis finally noticed that women on the physician-assisted side of his hospital died at a much higher rate than women on the side staffed by midwives. Without any knowledge of bacteria or viruses, he surmised that the doctors were passing on the contagion on their hands. Semmelweis insisted that physicians wash their hands in disinfectant solution between patients. Though his experiments proved he was right, Semmelweis was ostracized by his colleagues for suggesting that physicians were the cause of the problem. Driven mad by the stress of his professional exile, he died in a mental hospital.

person's job to come in. Some hospitals will allow you to hang a "Do not disturb" sign on your door.

One person you probably *do* want in your room is your nurse. A nurse will be assigned to take care of both you and your baby. She's a valuable resource who can answer your questions and provide tips and tricks—for instance, about breast-feeding—if you need them.

Since your nurse changes with each shift, you may end up with lots of different advice on the same subjects from several different nurses. All the advice is good, and all of it is different. So if your nurses all tell you something different about breast-feeding, for example, you can pick and choose which pieces of advice you want to try, then experiment on your own and come up with your own strategies. This is what mothers have been doing for centuries: taking advice from experienced women and then modifying it to suit their own needs.

Gleaning Pearls of Wisdom

I met Sharon and Mike about 12 hours after their first baby, Josh, was born. Both parents were understandably thrilled and elated. When I visited the next day, Sharon was noticeably more weary-looking than on the first visit. Naturally, she hadn't slept much during the previous 24 hours. She was still thrilled with the baby, but she admitted to me that she was starting to feel overwhelmed. She had endured an onslaught of nurses, aides, and doctors, not to mention friends and family parading into the room, all giving her tons of advice, all of it different. Sharon was beginning to doubt that she knew enough to take responsibility for a tiny living person. I told Sharon that these thoughts almost always enter a new mother's head, even if only fleetingly. I explained that it's normal for a new mother to feel conflicted about having a baby at all, and I congratulated her for having the strength to admit her feelings. I told Sharon that what I observed of her and her baby suggested that she already knew more than she thought she did, and the rest she would learn from experience. As for the multiple streams of advice that felt so overwhelming to her, I suggested to Sharon that she glean whatever pearls of wisdom seemed to make the most sense to her and discard the rest!

During every shift the nurse will probably unwrap your baby and take her vital signs: listening to her heart and taking her temperature. Because she's taking vital signs it's easy to assume that taking vital signs is an important thing to do and something you should do when you go home. This is not true. Remember, hospitals are designed to take care of sick people, and nurses are trained to take the vital signs of the patients in their care, but you needn't copy taking your baby's temperature unless she looks or acts sick.

Hands-on Diaper Changing

A Tip from Dr Rob:

When our first child was born, a nurse taught me how to change his diaper. I was already a board-certified pediatrician so I knew how to change a diaper, but I was sleep-deprived and was appreciative of any help and advice I could get. The nurse placed a new diaper under the baby's tush, then smeared some Vaseline on the diaper and sealed up the diaper. At home several days later when I was changing a diaper, I dutifully placed a clean diaper under my baby's tush, smeared some Vaseline on the diaper... and stopped. Why was I putting the Vaseline on my son's diaper instead of directly on his rear end, where it belonged? And then it dawned on me: In the hospital, the nurse was not permitted to touch my son's buttocks and genitals in my presence, lest I be offended or otherwise put off. I learned from this experience that just because a nurse or a doctor does something to your baby in the hospital doesn't mean that you should do the same thing at home. It will help if you have a questioning attitude.

For first-time, breast-feeding moms, often the most important person for you is not a pediatrician but a lactation consultant, especially if you need help troubleshooting the mechanics in the first few days. Lactation consultants can be enormously helpful during that stressful first week. Maternity nurses and hospital-based pediatricians can connect you with lactation consultants outside the hospital for help when you get home. Many take cash and don't take insurance, but you can be sure the return on your investment will be well worth it.

The pediatrician's visit in the hospital

A pediatrician will probably visit you every day. Sometimes the pediatrician will be the one you chose to follow your child after you leave the hospital, but more often than not the physician will be assigned to you by the hospital. These days there's a good chance the physician will be a pediatric hospitalist whose job it is to take care of children in a hospital setting only.

Sometimes the pediatrician will examine your baby in the well-baby nursery while you are resting, but the doctor may also come by while your baby is in the room with you. If you are trying to feed your baby, or if you have just succeeded in getting your baby to sleep after struggling for what seemed like an entire night, it's okay to ask the pediatrician not to disturb you and your baby. Feeding and sleeping are more important; the doctor can come back another time. While the pediatrician is there, however, you can take advantage of his or her knowledge and ask questions about your baby. Maybe you noticed something on your baby's skin you want checked out. This would be a good time to ask.

What NOW?

Does Your Baby Need the Bilirubin Test?

In most states the bilirubin level will be measured on every baby born to determine if the level is safe for the baby, regardless of how yellow the baby looks. This is the recommendation of the American Academy of Pediatrics, even though the United States Preventive Services Task Force observed that there is not enough evidence to indicate that testing every baby is helpful. If you have questions about your baby's bilirubin level, ask the doctor what the number means for the baby and if repeat testing will make any difference in how the baby will be treated.

One thing the pediatrician will do is make sure you have an appointment with a doctor set up for after you get home. The American Academy of Pediatrics recommends that a baby be seen in a doctor's office within 48 hours of discharge from a maternity ward regardless of how many days you've already spent in the hospital. For example, if you've had a Cesarean section, you may have been in the hospital for four or even five days. You're likely exhausted and uncomfortable from your surgery, yet you will be asked to pack up and go back to the doctor within two days.

One reason for the early follow-up is to look at the baby's skin. Most babies get yellow (jaundiced) in the first couple days of life due to the level of a chemical called *bilirubin* in their skin. Babies that are breast-fed will be yellower than bottle-fed babies.

Bilirubin in high levels can be bad for babies' brains, especially for smaller babies, premature babies. and babies who have been sick in the first days of life. For most babies, however, especially bottle-fed babies and babies whose moms' milk is coming in, the bilirubin level will drop on its own. If the bilirubin level is too high, the doctor may recommend supplementing a breast-fed baby with formula or lowering the bilirubin level by exposing the baby to intense blue lights, which is called "phototherapy."

Sometimes the baby doesn't look jaundiced at all, she's feeding like a champ, and perhaps you've just had a C-section, but the doctor *still* asks you to see a pediatrician within two days. In cases like these it's okay to call the pediatrician and discuss whether you need to come in right away or whether you can have a few days to rest.

What the heck is that? First poops in the hospital

The first poop your baby makes is not like any other poop she'll ever make. It will be dark green or black and will have the consistency of hot asphalt. This is *meconium*, the collection of cells and digested material that has been brewing in your baby's gut throughout pregnancy. Once the baby is born, it's got to come out. Meconium is devilishly difficult to wipe off. Use a warm terrycloth washcloth or a wet-wipe. Don't be afraid to hurt the baby: Wipe that meconium off like you mean it! Just when you get really good at wiping off meconium, your baby's poop will already be transitioning into that familiar mustard-seed poop that most babies make.

Testing, testing

Hospitals in most states do a series of screening tests on new babies.

Hearing test: It turns out that in the first few days of life you can figure out if the electrical circuits that allow a baby to hear are working. Of course, if the baby startles when someone closes a door in your room, you know this already. Still, the test is simple, relatively fast, and noninvasive. It only involves placing two sensors on the baby's head and headphones on the baby's ears when the baby is quiet and sleeping. If the baby doesn't pass the test, it can be repeated in most ENT (ear, nose, and throat) offices after you go home from the hospital.

Newborn screen: In most states, a nurse will also prick your baby's heel to get a sample of blood to test for several inborn errors of metabolism that are best caught early so that they can be treated early. One of the tests is for a condition called *hypothyroidism*, which is not common but also not extremely rare. Hypothyroidism is a condition in which the baby is born with little or no function of the thyroid gland. If the baby's thyroid gland doesn't make enough thyroid hormone, her brain won't develop normally. In the past, babies with congenital hypothyroidism used to develop mental retardation. That is why congenital hypothyroidism used to be called *cretinism*. Now, with universal newborn screening and treatment of affected babies with thyroid hormone, cretinism has virtually vanished. These babies' growth and development is completely normal. So the newborn screen is well worth your while.

Blood sugar: Some hospitals also prick a baby's heel to check blood sugar, especially if the mom had gestational diabetes. This is a fairly common condition that your obstetrician would have tested for during pregnancy. In some pregnancies the mom's blood sugar rises along with the increased metabolic demands of pregnancy. Sometimes her pancreas can't keep up with both her and her developing baby. The baby's pancreas works fine, but the baby has gotten used to swimming around in high blood sugar for several months so her own pancreas is revved up. As soon as she's born, however, her blood sugar may drop suddenly because her pancreas is still working as hard as it was in the womb. This condition usually corrects quickly, but in the meantime your nurses will check your baby's sugar often to make sure she's getting enough sugar from milk. If not, they might supplement her with some sugar-water or formula.

If nurses and doctors are checking your baby's blood sugar often, it's okay to ask a nurse or pediatrician why this is happening. It may be that the test isn't needed as often or at all.

To test or not to test

These three tests are only the standard tests done in newborn nurseries. There might be other tests, X-rays, or ultrasounds that the pediatrician may want to do. In every case, it's perfectly okay to ask the doctor if the test is absolutely necessary. A good question to ask is, "Doctor, what are you going to do with the results of this test once you get them?" If the doctor doesn't have a satisfactory answer, it may be that the test isn't necessary. The test may be important but not necessary to do right after your baby is born and can safely be postponed until she is a little older.

For babies born outside a hospital

If your baby is born at home or at a birthing center, it's likely that the staff will perform substantially fewer tests. One exception is the state newborn screening test for several inborn errors of metabolism such as hypothyroidism. I highly recommend this test. The midwives I know who attend home births offer to return to the home to perform this test 24 hours after the baby is born.

A little off the top? Deciding whether to circumcise

If you've had a boy, the nurses and the doctors are going to ask you if you want your baby circumcised. For some religious faith communities there is no question: The baby gets circumcised because that's what your community has done for centuries. For others the decision to circumcise comes down to the parents' wishes. Here are some factors to consider.

- *You need to be on the same page.* If you and your partner can't agree on whether to circumcise, don't do it! It's an irreversible procedure. If circumcision is needed for medical reasons later in life (and these cases are rare), it's a fairly easy procedure even though it's in a sensitive area.

- *There's no medical reason to circumcise your son.* In the modern developed world, there is no increased risk of infection or any other negative outcome for an uncircumcised boy. It's not difficult to clean an uncircumcised penis, and there's no pressing need to begin cleaning beneath the foreskin in the first year of life.

- *If you decide in favor of circumcision, ask the doctor about local anesthesia during the procedure.* Some doctors prepare the foreskin using a topical anesthetic called EMLA. EMLA does a pretty poor job of anesthesia. Much more effective are tiny injections of Lidocaine (similar to Novocaine) to block the nerves to the area. By using these injections circumcision can be done without pain. Most baby boys who are properly anesthetized don't even cry during the procedure.

Hospital visits from friends and family: Free advice is worth what you pay for it

You'll probably be getting lots of visits from friends and family. All of them will shower you with warm wishes and congratulations, not to mention compliments on your beautiful baby. Many will bring presents (which is why you don't need to buy infant clothes for your own baby—let other people do that). Unfortunately, the other thing visitors bring is advice.

If you haven't already been bombarded with advice, you will start getting it now. If you have already been subjected to streams of unsolicited advice, it's going to get much worse. For the most part, your family and friends will appreciate that you as new parents are sleep-deprived and your heads are swimming. If so, they'll leave you alone for now. In general, it's okay to tell them that you're really tired and ask if they could please save the advice for after you get home. If you're afraid of sounding rude, just blame the doctor. Thank your friends and family very much but tell them that the doctor says you mustn't be overloaded with information.

Breast or Bottle: An Important Early Decision

By the time you've had your baby, you may have decided how you want to feed her. Whatever your decision prior to and even after having your baby, you should know that it's not too late now to change your mind. Unless you're dead set against breast-feeding, it won't hurt you or your baby to give it a try. Remember that there are many nurses and lactation consultants who can help you learn how to do it. Perhaps there are even experienced breast-feeders among your family and friends who can help you. You shouldn't feel you have to stop because of a lack of help.

There is no question that the weight of scientific evidence leans heavily toward breast-feeding. But if there are medical or psychological reasons why you can't, you should not be made to feel as though you're not doing the best you can for your baby. Formula is good. It's very good, in fact, but breast milk is better. Here are some reasons *not* to choose bottle over breast.

- *It's too difficult.* There are many resources out there to help you through the tough initial phases of breast-feeding. The La Leche League is just one of many pro-breastfeeding organizations that exist just to help new moms. Contrary to what you might have heard, LLL is not as militantly pro-breastfeeding as you might think. LLL and other breast-feeding resources are there only to help you.

- *My husband doesn't want me to.* We're adults here. We can talk. Your husband probably likes your breasts, and he doesn't like the idea of being prohibited from access to them, right? But in this pediatrician's view, that's a pretty bad reason not to breast-feed. You'll still have them when your baby weans; then your husband can have his turn. After all, you're going to teach your child to share some day—you might as well start practicing what you plan to preach.

- *I have to return to work soon.* That's okay. You can still breast-feed. Maybe you won't be able to do it as much or as often as if you were at home, but you can still make it happen. There are few things in life about which one can say that a little is better than nothing. Breast-feeding is one of those things. Even if you breast-feed for as short as a week, your baby will benefit. Don't forget you can pump. Frozen breast milk can last so long that you can keep it for most of the first year you'll be feeding it to your baby.

Feeding issues: The 10% solution

Newborn babies lose weight. They're designed to lose weight. Full-term babies are born with some excess weight that we expect they'll lose while they're waiting for mom's milk to come in. The bigger the baby, the more weight we expect the baby to lose. The weight loss usually levels off by the end of the first week; then weight starts to rise again by about one ounce per day. Typically, it takes two weeks for a baby to get back to her birth weight.

Unfortunately, many hospitals become fixated on 10% weight loss as a maximum. There is no scientific reason for this. The importance of the 10% weight loss threshold is entirely made-up. Nevertheless, should a baby dip below the 10% weight-loss mark, many hospitals will suggest that you supplement your baby with formula. This is not necessarily the right thing to do. It's important to consider all the circumstances, in other words, to appreciate the 10% weight loss in context. Is the baby nursing well? Is mom's milk in yet? Does the baby look vigorous and healthy? I recommend that you take all these factors into account along with the weight loss before deciding to supplement with formula.

Breast *and* bottle?

It's easy to assume that one has to choose either breast-feeding or formula-feeding exclusively, but this isn't true. You can breast-feed and formula-feed together without confusing your baby or messing up the process of making breast milk. Examine your reasons for wanting to do both. Do you want to do both because you're afraid you're not making enough milk? That's what lactation consultants are for! If you fear your supply isn't enough (it probably *is* enough!), a lactation consultant can help figure out if this is true and help you troubleshoot feeding problems. Do you want to give both breast and bottle because you'll be going back to work soon? Did you know that you can breast-feed exclusively until you go back to work? You don't need to worry about so-called nipple confusion. The bottom line is: Don't worry about giving both breast and bottle. Just don't do it because you feel like you need to.

More decisions: Which formula?

Most hospitals give free samples of ready-to-feed formulas. They don't do this because they feel one type of formula is better than another; they do this because the formula companies give them product to give to you. The companies would like your business, naturally, and there's no better time to lock in future consumers than the first few days of life. Formula companies also know that once your baby starts drinking a certain kind of formula, you won't be likely to switch formulas. You should know that most infant formulas are very similar, with only very subtle differences among them. Although some babies are choosy about which formula they'll drink, most babies grate-fully accept whatever you give them. So you needn't buy your baby the same formula they give you in the hospital.

Ready? Get Set, GO! Coming Home from the Hospital

In case you weren't totally overwhelmed with the reality of a tiny new member of your family, now you face a more overwhelming prospect: You have to go home.

Fortunately, you aren't going to need as much stuff for your baby as you think you'll need. The hospital will send you home with some of the essentials: some diapers, some samples of formula if you need them, and some receiving blankets (technically, the hospital doesn't give these away, but the blankets often end up coming home with new babies and no one is the wiser). Your baby will need a place to sleep. For the first several weeks, this will be a simple bassinet or "Moses basket." The most challenging new item may be the car seat.

The car seat challenge

There are a ton of different brands and types of car seats available for sale, and no one brand is superior. There are, however, some brands that don't test as well as others. *Consumer Reports* is a good resource to consult. Your baby should fit comfortably in the seat, and the straps should fit snuggly but not tightly around her. If the straps are snug and not tight, being in the car seat will not hurt your baby—she'll be able to breathe just fine. Your baby may cry the first time (sometimes every time) you put her into the car seat, but all babies eventually get used to it. Car seats should be placed in the back seat, preferably in the middle of the back seat, facing backward. Many car seats come with a base that remains in the car when you remove the seat. The base for the car seat should be firmly strapped in with seat belts. There should be little play when you try to jiggle the seat.

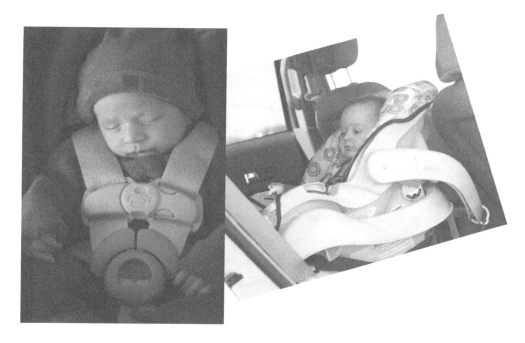

Babies need to ride in a rear-facing car seat (in the back seat of the car) until they are at least 20 pounds or one year old. The American Academy of Pediatrics suggests using rear-facing seats until age two. Make sure that the seat is installed properly according to the manufacturer's instructions. Check out the National Highway Traffic Safety Administration website (www.nhtsa.gov) for the Child Care Seat Inspection Station Locator to find a nearby inspection station where certified technicians will inspect your car seat and teach you how to install it safely—usually at no charge.

Wrestling Your Car Seat into Submission

Follow the manufacturer's installation instructions for your car seat to the letter and install it when you've had a good night's sleep. I learned from bitter experience how difficult the installation can be when you're sleep-deprived. If you have trouble installing your car seat (and most people do), many local police or fire departments can help you install it or verify that you've installed it correctly. Having said this, a safe car seat is a car seat that is installed in a vehicle that is driven safely. Observe the speed limits and stop at stop signs. That's why they're there.

Dressing your baby to leave the hospital

Few parents underdress their babies to leave the hospital. To the contrary: Most parents put way too much clothing on their babies before going outside, particularly in the winter. The rule of thumb is that your baby should wear one more layer than you wear when you go outside. In any case, your baby is better off wearing a hat than extra layers, since it's much easier for a baby to lose heat from her head than for an adult-sized person. Some parents also throw a receiving blanket over the baby carrier to shield the baby from sun or wind or from well-wishers who may want to touch her (this is yet another way those receiving blankets seem to escape from hospitals).

Aim for an inside temperature between 68 and 72 degrees Fahrenheit. If you can sustain this temperature, then your baby will only need to wear a "onesie" and a hat and be wrapped in a single blanket. If it gets colder than 68 degrees in your house or apartment, dress your baby in an uncomplicated set of pajamas. By uncomplicated, I mean not too many snaps. Please pity those among us who are completely useless when it comes to outfits with snaps!

If your baby is hot, she'll probably sweat. It's not a good idea to overdress or overswaddle a baby. If your baby sweats, dress her in one less layer. If your baby is cold, she'll probably cry. Another way to tell if she's cold is to look at her skin. A cold baby may have cold hands and feet, or a lacy blue pattern called "mottling" may appear on her body and extremities. If your baby is mottled, add another layer.

All This Stuff Is New: Key Tips for New Parents

Most new parents believe there's a ton of information they need to know before leaving the hospital. The truth is that there is only a small handful of tips and tricks to keep in mind. The nurses and doctors in the hospital will probably give a quick rundown as you're struggling to pack your bags. Here's a summary of what they might say.

The umbilical stump

A nurse likely will cut off the plastic umbilical cord clip before you go home. If she hasn't, it's not a big deal, but please don't try to cut it off yourself—you need a special tool. Umbilical cords usually fall off after about two weeks. Some fall off earlier; others fall off later.

When umbilical cords start to fall off, they'll bleed a little or ooze slightly. They often stain the baby's onesie or T-shirt. This is normal. The care of the umbilical stump has changed quite a bit over the years. The current recommendation is to leave the stump alone and to let it dry in the air. This will help it fall off more quickly. Avoid getting the stump wet since wetting it will delay the process of falling off. When the stump falls off altogether, you can give your baby a tub bath.

Speaking of the tub...

Babies don't get dirty. They don't go outside and play in the dirt. The parts of the baby that do get dirty get cleaned 8 to 12 times a day (when you change diapers). Baby skin has lots of nice natural oils in it, just as all skin does. When you bathe a baby, you wash away the oils as well as the dirt. A typical baby does well with one tub bath per week. Second or third children sometimes get bathed even less often for reasons that

The History of Umbilical Cord Care

The earliest texts on care of the newborn recommended rolling babies in salt without any explanation. The authors of these texts simply observed that babies rolled in salt tended to survive the first few days of life better than non-salted babies. It was probably the antiseptic properties of salt that kept babies from acquiring infections, most likely through the umbilicus, one of the most vulnerable sites for infection. In the twentieth century until the 1970s, when mothers and babies typically stayed in the hospital for up to ten days following birth, the practice was to refrain from bathing the baby until the day before going home. Since hospitals were (and still are) veritable Petri dishes of bacteria, babies frequently contracted bacterial infections of the umbilical cord during these long hospital stays. As a result, some hospitals started bathing babies in antiseptic solutions, and the rates of infection dropped. Unfortunately, the antiseptic baths were toxic, so the practice was discontinued. In the 1970s, hospital staff began painting "triple dye," usually containing Iodine or Gentian Violet, on the umbilical stump to prevent infection. This was the standard of care until fairly recently. Today, in the era of universal precautions regarding hand-washing and awareness of potentially infected surfaces, we tend to treat umbilical cords with benign neglect, watching them carefully for swelling and redness that may indicate infection and applying antibiotic ointments such as Neosporin if such signs appear. It's far more sensible than rolling a baby in salt.

will become obvious once you have your hands full with more than one child. As my wife used to say about our second child, "He gets a bath once a week, if he's lucky."

It's always a good idea after a bath to slather on some hypoallergenic moisturizer. Your baby will love the massage, and you'll keep the skin nice and moist. In full-term babies, and especially in post-dates (overdue) babies, the skin tends to peel a lot (I joke that all babies, at some level, are reptiles). For reasons that are not entirely clear, many hospitals don't permit you to moisturize your baby's peeling skin. But as soon as you get home feel free to moisturize away.

Guarding the family jewels: Circumcision care

If your baby boy had a circumcision in the hospital, you're going to want to know how to care for it at home. First, a quick public service announcement for new dads: Guys, even a good circumcision looks awful. They're supposed to look bad. Now you will reasonably ask: What does a *bad* circumcision look like? Never mind that.

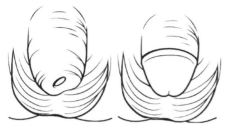

A circumcision (right-hand image) heals over several days. Slathering the site with petroleum jelly will help.

A "freshly minted" circumcision is going to look red or purple and angry. There will be a ring of swollen tissue right at the cut surface. A couple of days later, there will be a white or yellow film that appears around the newly exposed head. This is entirely normal. It doesn't mean the penis is infected.

We recommend that you slather the site with petroleum jelly for seven days after the circumcision every time you change the diaper. Don't worry about getting poop on the site—it will *not* get infected. Regular petroleum jelly will do; you don't need to use an antibiotic ointment even if the hospital sends you home with a tube of the stuff. The point is to keep the healing circumcision from sticking to the diaper. After seven days the ring of tissue will still be swollen, but the circumcision will be healed enough that there will be nothing left to stick to the diaper and you can stop the petroleum jelly routine. As always, don't be afraid to clean the circumcision.

Skin stuff

Lots of things can and will appear on your baby's skin. In Appendix A I summarize some of the most common skin rashes you may encounter on your baby during the first six months.

What's that noise?

Babies make a lot of odd noises. There are a couple of reasons why the sounds that come out of your baby sound so strange. First, your baby's nose and the back of her throat are small and relatively floppy. When your baby sleeps, these already small and floppy structures get smaller and floppier. When a baby tries to breathe through a small narrow space, she's going to make a noise that can sound like a squeak or a wheeze. These sounds are normal.

Charting Pees and Poops

Many hospitals will send you home with a chart that allows you to record how often your baby has had a wet and/or dirty diaper as well as a chart for how often she has fed (and on which side, if you're breast-feeding). Most of these charts are unnecessary. Charting dirty diapers is fraught with complications. For example, if you change your baby before she's done pooping, is that one dirty diaper or two? And if the diaper is heavy with baby poop, should you count that as a wet diaper as well?

There's a much easier rule of thumb to follow: Your baby will poop about one time for every time you feed her. In general, it's much more important to pay attention to what goes into your baby than what comes out. In other words, keep track of feeding. How well your baby feeds is the single best and most sensitive indicator of how well your baby is doing. So toss out the charts, and pay attention to your baby!

When your baby goes to feed, she'll make a lot of noise since that small and floppy area is now sharing space with milk she's swallowing. She may snort like a pig. As long as she can feed comfortably, there's no reason to try to clear out a baby's nose. Only if your baby can't nurse and breathe at the same time is it worth the effort to try to suction her nose out with that bulb you brought back from the hospital.

Your baby will hiccup as well. Hiccups are perfectly normal, and many moms notice that their baby hiccups a lot in the womb. Babies that hiccup a lot inside tend to hiccup a *ton* outside. A hiccup is triggered every time the baby swallows anything, be it milk or air. It's not because the baby is cold or because she ate too fast. And don't say "boo" to the baby or have her drink upside-down. That won't get rid of hiccups.

Babies also sneeze a lot. It doesn't mean they're sick or allergic. Most of the time, sneezing is a reflex triggered by looking at lights. All babies have this reflex. Most of them shed it by about two months of age; some hold onto it for life. These are the adults who need to look at light to sneeze.

Pacifiers

First, a confession: I'm a big fan of the pacifier, up to a point. Prior to four months of age, a baby really needs something outside her body to help soothe her. Most babies satisfy this need to be soothed by sucking, and if they cannot suck on a pacifier they will use mom as a pacifier. Our second child did this for a year. My wife reports it was annoying, to say the least. If you plan to breast-feed exclusively, and your baby won't take a pacifier at first, don't give up. Try different sizes and shapes. If you hit on something she likes you'll be glad you made the effort. Just be sure you throw away the pacifier at six months. If you keep it in longer than that, it will become a habit that some day you may regret not breaking sooner.

What about *You?*

If all this information seems overwhelming to you, you're in good company. It *can* be overwhelming. Getting to know your new baby can be both enormously awe-inspiring and incredibly scary. It's important to remember through all this that the path you're taking is well worn. New parents have been taking it for millennia; they survived and so will you. If you feel as though you can't handle the journey on your own, *ask for help.* Humans are social animals. We live in groups for a reason: We need each other's help. You may need help buying food and household essentials, doing the laundry, or even just cleaning up around the house. It's no failure on your part to ask family and friends to do things for you during those stressful first days and weeks. To the contrary: That's what family and friends are for. Go ahead and ask.

It's also quite normal for moms (and dads) to get the Baby Blues. Even though post-partum depression is an official diagnosis, if you're feeling down in the days and weeks following bringing your baby home, it doesn't mean something is wrong with you or that you need to take medication. This is a normal reaction following the stress of childbirth and confrontation with the awesome responsibility of raising a child. It's never easy for *any* new parent.

What you need is the love and support of your partner, your family, your friends, and your community. If you don't have these resources to help you, ask the nurses at the hospital or your pediatrician for recommendations of places where you can get the support and the help you need.

Chapter Highlights

- What makes your baby tick?
- What can she do? What does she do?
- What can you do with her?
- What do your baby's cues mean?

Chapter 2

Getting to Know Your Baby

Now that you're home from the hospital and you're getting ready to adjust to your radically changed life, you may begin to ask yourselves some questions: Just who is this little person in my house? What is my baby going to be like? Can she see and hear? What else can she do? What should or shouldn't I be doing with her? Let's get to know her.

How a Baby Is Like a Pinball Machine

Babies arrive fully loaded. They are born with all the capabilities of a human being. They only need a dozen years of love, care, and feeding to develop into complete people. But not every system works the way an adult's does, or even the way an older infant's does.

Take the sensory organs, for example. All five of a baby's senses work: sight, hearing, taste, smell, and touch. The problem with newborns is that all five senses are working all the time, and the baby cannot filter out any of the sensory data. To explain further: The reason you are able to read this book is that you are able to filter out most of the sensory inputs that are coming your way. You don't pay attention to the lights in the room or to extraneous sounds coming from outside. You probably are also filtering out the feel of the book in your hands as well as the scents around you and the taste in your mouth. Now imagine that you are forced to pay attention to all these sensations equally. If you were, you'd be incapacitated. You'd be forced to put the book down and go lie in bed. This is what the world is like for a newborn. Fortunately, newborns are lying down already.

This is why most babies prefer low-sensory environments. They do well in places where there isn't too much light, noise, and temperature fluctuation. They tend to prefer dim lighting, near silence, and contact with warm human bodies. We can tell that babies prefer these conditions and do well in them because they eat and sleep better than in noisy, light, cold, and hot environments.

Because babies are unable to filter out sensory stimulation, they've developed a way to protect themselves from overstimulation. I call it the "tilt" function. In the era of desktop-based and hand-held gaming, fewer and fewer people remember old-school arcade pinball machines, complete with silver-ball plunger, electronic bumpers, and flashing lights. Classic pinball machines all came equipped with a "tilt" feature, which prevented you from cheating by jiggling the machine to make the ball go where you wanted. If you jiggled the machine, a "tilt" light came on, the machine went to sleep, and you lost the ball.

A baby's "tilt" function is not so dramatic. In fact, most parents never see it in action. They only find out about it after the fact. For example, if parents take their newborn to a Labor Day picnic with lots of people and loud music and smells from the barbecue, afterward they might turn to each other and say, "Wow, our baby was so GOOD! She slept through the entire picnic. "

Well, of course the baby slept through the entire picnic: She was overstimulated! She responded to all this stimulation by going "tilt" and shutting down. In this way she protected herself from becoming overwhelmed with all the sensory inputs coming her way. Parents often find out just how overstimulated their baby is when she becomes incredibly fussy later—after the sensory overload—when she has difficulty going to sleep or even feeding. For this reason, I recommend that parents of newborns avoid overstimulating environments, such as holiday celebrations.

Your Newborn: A Bundle of Infantile Reflexes

Remember that your baby is a fully functional human being with an unfortunate lack of ability to filter sensations. Otherwise, your baby is a real person. Another major difference between a baby and an adult is that a baby is a bundle of infantile reflexes that interfere with her ability to coordinate her actions and to interact with you. You may have heard of some of these reflexes: the startle reflex, the *Moro reflex* (it looks like the baby is trying to grab hold of the air), the tonic neck posture (aka the "fencer's pose"), and so on. If it weren't for all these immature reflexes, your baby would be much better able to move purposefully and to interact with you. There are a lot of things a baby would probably like to do but can't because she's just too uncoordinated!

Moro reflex: The newborn Moro reflex, also called the "startle reaction," causes a baby that suddenly feels as if it's dropping to spread its arms. A loud noise or even a change in temperature can also trigger the reaction.

Stepping reflex: If you hold an infant younger than two months upright and touch her feet to a surface, she will automatically "step," putting one foot ahead of the other.

Grasping reflex: Anything that touches a baby's palm will elicit a grasping reflex, which can be surprisingly strong.

Even though your baby is held captive by a bunch of infantile reflexes, inside is a fully alert person who is paying attention to her environment. She's capable of feeling happiness, pain, hunger, cold, warmth, and pleasure, even though it appears that she just lies there, cries, and eats. The things she's paying attention to are *cues*. She needs cues to learn how she's supposed to act in this world: Should I be afraid of this world? Should I cry a lot? Or should I feel reassured and safe in my mother's and my father's arms, knowing everything is going to be all right?

The way your baby asks questions is by crying. Your baby always cries because she needs something. She could be hungry, she could have a gas bubble or a wet diaper, or she could just want to be held. She needs to get a specific response from you to feel that her needs are being addressed.

A baby can tell if you're stressed. She can feel it in your muscle tone. She can smell it in your sweat. And if you're stressed, she's going to be stressed. So how do you avoid giving her the cue that she should be stressed? It's not easy, but try to *act* as if you're cool, calm, and collected. Pretending can help you *be* calm, cool, and collected.

Two Studies in Body English

Most first-time parents are nervous, and Rebecca was no different. She had a lot of reasons to be nervous. She and her husband Sam had been trying for years to have a baby. After a long and exhaustive series of fertility tests and treatments, they finally made the difficult (and expensive) decision to pursue *in vitro* fertilization (IVF). Rebecca and Sam's baby, David, was born full-term and healthy when mom and dad were both 39 years old.

All babies are precious, but David was especially precious because of all the time and tears that had been spent bringing him into the world. Rebecca was especially nervous that something would go horribly wrong with her perfectly healthy baby, so she was particularly disturbed when David cried. Rebecca picked him up with stiff arms, bounced him a bit vigorously, and spoke to him in a loud, almost panicked voice. This method seldom calmed David down.

As David grew into a toddler, I found him to be an unusually skittish child. He felt easily threatened and cried when strangers approached him. As he grew and as his parents became more comfortable with David falling down and getting bruised, David began to absorb the blows from the slings and arrows that life flung at him without exploding in tears. The arrival of his brother Eric when David was two and a half made a huge difference in David's life.

Though Eric was also conceived via IVF, Rebecca and Sam were much calmer parents the second time around. At his one-month visit, Rebecca said to me, "You know, we really lucked out this time! This baby is so much calmer and quieter than David was. He eats better, he sleeps better, and you can lay him in the bouncy seat, and he just happily plays there. He only cries when he's hungry."

I told Rebecca and Sam that in almost every family I hear the same story with second-time parents. I told them that luck has little to do with how "easy" the baby is. Rebecca and Sam deserve the credit. The parents had communicated signals to baby Eric through their body language. Mom and dad were relaxed when they held him: Eric got the message. Babies pay attention to these things. As a side effect of this turn of events, David himself began to relax and handle what life threw at him much more calmly.

If your baby senses that you're on top of things and you know what you're doing, she says to herself, "Okay, mom and dad are cool, so I'm cool too." These babies eat better, sleep better, and appear to be happy babies. But you can see how easily the wheel can turn in the other direction. If you feel as if your colicky baby is making you stressed, and in turn your stress is making your colicky baby more colicky, you can see how things can spin out of control. You want to try to stop the wheel and turn it around. Here's how.

Take a break. If there is anyone who can come over and take care of your baby, invite that person over. Then leave the house or apartment. You should go for a walk, to the gym, to the salon, to the movies—anything to give you time and space to breathe and to consider how far you've come in such a short time.

Find someone to tell you you're doing a great job as a parent. All parents need someone to tell them this. If you don't have anyone in your life to tell you you're doing a great job, you should tell yourself. Try it. It works!

In general, less is more when it comes to babies: less sound, less light, less stimulation, and if humanly possible, less stress.

What Can My Baby See?

I get a ton of questions about a newborn baby's ability to see. This is probably because many parents notice that their babies aren't looking straight at them, even when mom holds her baby in front of her face. The problem is coordination.

There are no fewer than six extraocular muscles in each eye tasked with the responsibility of rotating the eyeball around a central point in an attempt to aim the pupil at an object of interest. This doesn't include the muscles attached to the lens that help focus the image on the back of your eye. A newborn baby doesn't have the necessary coordination to work all the muscles in both eyes properly. That's why babies' eyes often drift in different directions like a gecko's.

That's not to say that your baby's eyes don't work properly. On the contrary, if you position yourself 12 inches from your baby's face and if neither of you move, your baby can focus on you fairly well. This usually lasts only a few seconds, though, as one of you will move or one of your baby's eye muscles will tire and she will lose the image. Keeping an object in one's gaze takes skills; so does sharply focusing on an object. It takes about two months before even a well-focused object looks sharp in a baby's eyes. But your baby can see the things that are important for her to see: your smile, your eyes, and some of the features of your face. By eight months of age, a baby's visual acuity is as good as it's going to get.

By the end of the second month, your baby's coordination will be so much better that she'll be able to track you with her eyes as you walk across the room. Lying on her back, she may be able to track a relatively slow-moving object through a 180-degree arc.

Is it true that newborns can only see black and white? No. What *is* true is that babies seem to be fascinated by high-contrast images, black and white images being an obvious example. But babies can see color. There is even some suggestion that babies' color vision improves more quickly than the overall sharpness of their vision.

It's well known that four-month-olds can bat at nearby interesting objects, and that six-month-olds can reach purposefully for objects. Some experts believe that these skills appear because the baby can see objects better at four months and even better at six months. The truth is more complicated. Older babies are more coordinated overall than two-month-olds. They bat and reach for objects because they are better coordinated to do so, not because they can see them better. The truth is probably that babies from the earliest days find objects near them (particularly parents' faces) interesting; it's just that they can't get their coordination together to reach for those objects of fascination.

What *should* a baby look at?

We return to the theme of low stimulation. Babies get a lot more information out of objects that are uncomplicated: simple lines and simple colors that are easy to understand. The ideal object is the human face, gazing lovingly at the baby. You accomplish two important goals simultaneously by gazing at your baby: You help stimulate your baby's vision, and you establish a close human interaction.

One-month-old babies seem fascinated with many seemingly boring objects. For example, a one-month-old will stare at the lights for minutes at a time. (Don't worry, she won't damage her eyes.) Babies also seem interested in painted walls. I believe this is because, for a baby, all these things are new—and interesting.

Between two and six months, babies appear to love handling objects like toys as a way of exploring and learning about the world and of sharing the experience with the person to whom they've bonded.

The Social Smile

Even though babies are born with less-than-perfect coordination, and though their movements are impeded by a slew of infantile reflexes, it's important to remember that each baby is a real person whose brain is able to adopt that subjective emotion—now what's it called? You know, when you feel really good and all's well with the world? Oh, yes! *Happiness.* Your baby can feel happy even when she can't show it to the world. Your baby will feel like smiling when anybody would feel like smiling: When gazing into her mother's face, when she's getting a nice massage, when she's being sung to. The smiles, I tell new parents, are inside your baby. It just takes more effort on her part to get them out in the first few weeks.

We don't need to think about smiling. We do it reflexively. No one has to teach you to smile. It is a human response to pleasurable stimuli. Smiles start in the brain with the subjective feeling of happiness. They get processed through a complex series of neurological events that we don't completely understand and are transmitted to the muscles in our faces, and we smile.

The challenge for babies is getting the smile from the frontal cortex of the brain to the muscles in the cheeks. Smiling, like focusing the eyes, requires a complex feat of coordination that we take for granted but that a baby is just getting used to. Most babies will smile in response to your smiling face at about six to eight weeks. We call this the "social smile."

Many parents tell me they see their baby smile earlier than this—or maybe it was a smile, maybe it was gas. I tell parents a smile is a smile. The smiles are in there, I remind parents. Sometimes the baby gets lucky and the smile sneaks out.

If you don't see the social smile at six to eight weeks, it's not necessarily a cause for worry. Nevertheless, if you're worried about it, please bring your concern to your pediatrician. The social smile, like all developmental milestones, must be appreciated in the context of all the other growth and developmental parameters. That is to say, by itself the social smile is a special, endearing sign of development, but it must be appreciated in the context of everything else your baby is doing.

Interacting with Your Newest Family Member

Okay, keep it simple for your baby. Low stimulation, low stress—no barbecues. So what *can* you do with your baby? Not much. Newborn babies mostly eat and sleep. A normal newborn baby will sleep 20 hours per day and will spend the other four hours eating and being changed. There's not time for much else except for connecting, and there's plenty of time for that.

The gaze: Bonding with your baby

We can't perform detailed psychological testing on babies. They can't fill out questionnaires. We can only guess about what works well when it comes to bonding with a baby. The best advice I can give is not so much derived from science as it is based on a common-sense understanding of several millennia of parents raising children.

The good news is that, in general, there isn't any special skill or knowledge involved in bonding with a baby. The best way to do it is to do things you're going to do anyway and hold and talk to your baby. New parents often ask me what the best things are that they can do to help their baby to develop. I tell them to hold the baby and talk to her. "That's it?" they respond, incredulously. Yes. That's it.

You may already be falling in love with this little person you created. For most parents, it's easy to look at her as though you love her. I acknowledge that sometimes it takes time to fall in love. You may be feeling ambivalent about her at first. This is normal. It's important to pay attention to your feelings.

We can't know for sure, but to the extent that your baby can focus on your face (discussed later in this chapter), she can recognize your loving expression and intuitively understand what it means. Babies look to us for cues for how to behave in this world. It's okay to be unsure of your feelings, but try to smile anyway. You might start feeling the feelings that the smile suggests. Like all of the relationships in our lives, sometimes even the mother-baby relationship requires work.

How Science Views the Parent-Baby Bond

Babies and parents have been bonding with each other since the dawn of time, but until the early twentieth century no one tried to understand the nature of the bond or to describe its development.

Sigmund Freud (1856–1939) was perhaps the most famous theorist to examine the maternal-infant relationship in a systematic way. Freud's insights began with the commonplace observation that infants obtain satisfaction from sucking (after all, they have to eat!). Freud referred to this period of life as the "Oral Stage," and argued (implausibly, in my opinion) that frustrations of a baby's oral drives would lead to neuroses in adulthood.

Apart from his theories (now largely discredited) regarding the infant's loving attachment to the mother's breast, Freud had little or nothing to say about the developing relationship between mother and baby. He was more interested in how early childhood traumas, particularly sexual abuse, gave rise to disturbances later in life.

Erik Erikson (1902–1994) was a developmental psychologist most famous for coining the often-misunderstood expression "identity crisis." But Erikson should be better known for his division of psychological development into a series of conflict resolutions. For our purpose, a discussion of infants, the conflict Erikson was interested in was the conflict between *trust* and *mistrust*.

According to Erikson, the major developmental task for an infant is to learn whether or not her parents will satisfy her basic needs. If parents are consistent sources of food, comfort, and affection, an infant learns trust—that others are dependable and reliable. If her parents are neglectful, the infant instead learns mistrust—that the world is an undependable place. Although it is negative, having some experience with mistrust enables the older child and adult to deal with uncertainty and unpredictability.

My own view of Erikson's theory is that all of Erikson's conflict stages can be lumped into one: dependence versus independence. Infancy certainly is a stage where dependence wins: The infant is entirely dependent on adults for her very life, and for the most part, she accepts her dependence. And parents readily and enthusiastically accept the role of provider for the baby's needs.

Jean Piaget (1896–1980) was a Swiss developmental psychologist and philosopher. He is best known for creating the study of cognitive development in children from birth onward. Piaget's major insight was that infants must start life *egocentric* in order to end up *sociocentric*. In other words, it is absolutely necessary for an infant to begin life totally focused on her viewpoint, without regard for others' (including those of her parents). This is a necessary step, Piaget argued, for a child to develop into a well-adjusted socially aware adult. Piaget might argue that the infant develops the ability to bond with her parents by developing her abilities to have her needs met.

(continued)

Another important contribution of Piaget was his *theory of object permanence*. Object permanence is just the realization that objects exist when the baby can't see them. Most babies, however, don't understand object permanence until they are nine months old. This means that, until the baby is nine months old, when mom and dad walk out of the room they cease to exist for the baby! Clearly, for the baby bonding is difficult with a person whose reality comes and goes at a moment's notice. In fact, Piaget was not interested in parental-infant bonding in the sense we understand it.

John Bowlby (1907–1990), a British psychologist, picked up where Piaget left off and attempted to create a theory of parental-infant bonding that occurs once the infant develops object permanence, at about nine months of age. Bowlby became interested in child psychology in the aftermath of World War II, studying children who had been orphaned during the London Blitz. Observing that many of these children developed severe psychological disturbances, Bowlby hypothesized that the cause might have been their early loss of contact with their mothers. Bowlby developed his hypothesis into what became known as *the attachment theory*, which states that, for an infant to develop socially and emotionally, she needs to form a relationship with at least one primary caregiver.

Bowlby's work rested on the assumption that infants are born with the ability and the desire to attach to a caregiver. This point of view was challenged in the 1960s by the *theory of behaviorism*, which suggested bonding was a behavior that had to be taught to an infant. Subsequent research proved that Bowlby was right: Infants, and many higher animals as well, possess an inborn capacity to bond with a caring adult.

T. Berry Brazelton (1918–) is a pediatrician who studies the bonding abilities of infants, including premature infants, from the earliest days of life. Brazelton's major contribution was the idea that infants are born fully equipped with many capabilities that allow them to interact with their world, by which he meant a baby's parents. Brazelton showed that babies communicate their needs by using a "rational language," though it might not seem like a language. After all, the baby isn't communicating by using words. Finally, in the process of creating a bond with parents, Brazelton showed that infants not only give cues to parents about what they need but also respond to cues from their parents about how to act in the world. For example, if the parents are calm and confident, they communicate this calmness and confidence to the baby by their body language. In response, the baby, if she could speak, would say, "Okay, Mom and Dad are cool, so I guess I'll be cool too."

Baby talk

I admit a bias against baby talk. It makes no sense to the baby anyway, so why do people do it? Because people think they should talk baby talk to babies. Fortunately, this rule was never written down or etched in stone on a mountain. For example, there's no need to refer to yourself as "mommy" or "daddy," or to refer to your baby by her name when addressing her. It's perfectly okay to use the pronouns "I" and "you." Remember, your baby doesn't understand what you're saying anyway. It's the tone, the expression, and the body language that she's paying attention to.

All this is not to suggest that you speak to your baby the way you speak to your friends or to the UPS guy. Of course you're going to speak gently and lovingly to her. You kiss and snuggle with her to let her know you mean what you say. Babies don't understand the words, but they're very good at getting the gist.

AKA Snookums

We've all witnessed parents who forget to *stop* talking baby talk to their children, as in this old yarn. A mother is fussing over her five-year-old before he's shipped off to the first day of kindergarten. "Does Snookums want Mommy to carry Snookums's lunchbox for Snookums? Or does Snookums want to carry it? Does Snookums want a kiss from Mommy? MWAH! Make sure Snookums has a good first day of Kindergarten. Mommy loves Snookums."

At the end of the day, the boy returns to the kitchen. His mother is overjoyed. "Snookums! Does Snookums want to tell Mommy what Snookums learned the first day of kindergarten?"

Her child replies, "I learned my name was Marvin."

I promise that if you begin speaking standard English to your baby and if you use pronouns correctly, nothing bad will happen. To the contrary: When your child learns to speak, she just might speak grammatically correct English!

Since your baby is reading only the emotional, relational content of the interaction, what you talk about doesn't matter. You could be reciting passages from *Julius Caesar*; it would make no difference. Your baby would continue to pay rapt attention and enjoy fixing on your loving gaze. I remember reading *The Wind in the Willows* to my boys when they were too young to understand it. But that made no difference to them. The language sounded beautiful, and the reading provided an opportunity for bonding between the boys and me. That's what counted.

Similarly, when talking to your baby, the subject matter needn't consist of baby talk. As long as the tone is gentle and loving, you can talk about your day with her or give a running commentary of what's happening while you're changing her diaper. She'll return your gaze and smile, and you will have accomplished an important goal—making a connection with your child. In so doing, you teach your baby that this is how humans interact: We look each other in the eyes and speak kindly to one another.

Baby-sing

For reasons that no one has figured out, people love music, particularly the sound of the human voice singing. Babies are no exception. It is said: "Music hath charms that soothe a savage breast." And while we recoil from referring to our babies as savages, we intuit that babies are complete yet unformed people, in a primitive state. Yet music affects them in much the same way it stirs us. Music calms nerves, excites emotions, and helps create bonds between people.

It doesn't matter if you can't sing. Babies don't seem to care if you can carry a tune. They only care that you are singing a song, and they immediately become enthralled. The choice of song doesn't seem to matter much either, though you're much more likely to deliver the kind of message you want by singing a "nice" song. Love songs work well, particularly old ones. We sang Cole Porter's "Our Love is Here to Stay" to the boys as they lay in their cribs. When they began to speak, they requested the song by name. Some families sing religious songs they bring from their houses of worship. Others choose songs from movies.

Whatever you say or sing to your baby, remember: be gentle and loving. The recommendation stems in part from our earlier discussion of the importance of low stimulation in a baby's world. Soft, gentle reminders of how beautiful you think your baby is tend to work better than blow-by-blow descriptions of arguments you had at work that day. "Come Away With Me" by Norah Jones tends to sit better with an infant at bedtime than Nirvana's "Smells Like Teen Spirit."

Bonding with dad

For fathers especially, your newborn's virtually exclusive eat-sleep schedule can be disconcerting. I remember thinking of my newborn boys as essentially uninteresting human beings, *and I was a board-certified pediatrician!* I should have known better. How much greater this feeling of frustration must be for normal dads.

That doesn't mean that a father is essentially useless for his newborn. To the contrary: Dad is extremely important for both baby and for mom, especially in the early days. That's why, if at all possible, it would be great if dad could get a week or two off from work to stay at home with mom and their baby.

There are many ways in which dad can bond with the baby and give mom the help she needs—short of actually feeding the baby. The first thing he can do is realize that mom is probably enormously tired and stressed out from the experience of giving birth. She needs lots of help. In general, if the task involves getting up from the bed or the couch, it would be great if someone could do it for her: getting water, clean diapers, wipes, her laptop, her cell phone, or anything she needs. I have lots of moms in my practice who insist on cooking and cleaning when they get home from the hospital. I have never understood this. Why would you want to become more stressed than you already are? See if you can get dad to do it.

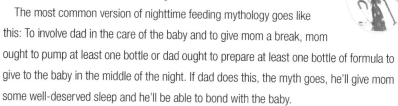

The Nighttime Bottle Fallacy

A Tip from Dr Rob:

The most common version of nighttime feeding mythology goes like this: To involve dad in the care of the baby and to give mom a break, mom ought to pump at least one bottle or dad ought to prepare at least one bottle of formula to give to the baby in the middle of the night. If dad does this, the myth goes, he'll give mom some well-deserved sleep and he'll be able to bond with the baby.

It never works this way. In my experience, mom never sleeps through the nighttime feeding, thereby obviating one of the main reasons for pumping. To make matters worse, she's wasted some of her precious time and energy during that pumping session that she could have spent more profitably giving milk directly to her baby. And the bonding that supposedly happens never seems to balance out the disruption in the baby's normal routine.

Instead, in many families dad gets up, picks up and changes the baby, and brings her to mom to feed. If and only if mom is going to sleep through this process, dad can prepare a bottle of formula or thaw some pumped breast milk. If mom isn't sleeping and she is breast-feeding, it might just be easier for everybody, especially her baby, if she does the feeding.

With the possible exception of Freud, no twentieth-century expert on bonding suggests that there is something particular to mom that precludes the baby bonding with dad. Bowlby, for example, would argue that as long as the baby has consistent, stable contact with her father, she will identify him as a caregiver and seek attachment with him for satisfaction of her needs.

My experience with infants in the office is that once they develop object permanence (definitely by nine months), they begin to gravitate toward dad as well as mom preferentially over any stranger (especially the pediatrician). As long as their parents are close by, most infants will warm up to a stranger after a few minutes and even allow a

What NOW?

Daddy's Girl

Laura is the only daughter in a family that has been with me since I began my practice. At that time, the Tech Bubble had just burst. Laura's dad, Carson, who had been employed as an engineer at one of the many software companies west of Boston, lost his job. Carson's layoff occurred the week Laura was born. Laura's mother, Rima, was an in-house attorney at a financial services company. Rima's benefit package allowed her to stay home for 12 weeks per the Family and Medical Leave Act.

At this point, Carson and Rima had to make a decision: What would they do with Laura when Rima had to go back to work? Would they put Laura in daycare while Carson looked for a job? The problem was there were no software jobs to be found, so Carson became a stay-at-home dad.

The plan had been that Carson would look for a job when the economy improved, but weeks stretched into months, and Carson was enjoying taking care of Laura at home. Rima had a good job, and it didn't make financial sense for them to put Laura in daycare when Carson could stay at home with her.

Laura is now nine years old and in third grade, and Carson still hasn't gone back to work. Instead, he works as hard as he did at his old job. He has taken Laura to every well-child visit since she was born. Carson sends me emails with non-urgent questions and pages me with the urgent ones. I can count on one hand the number of times I've spoken to Rima in nine years.

Laura is a highly intelligent, funny, and engaging little girl. From all appearances, her social and emotional development is normal. For Carson and Rima, circumstances dictated who was going to stay at home and care for their baby. For Laura, all that mattered was that at least one of her parents has been there for her entire life.

stranger to hold them. Very soon, however, the infant will protest for return to her mother's or her father's arms.

The forgotten bond: Mom and dad

While all this discussion about bonding with baby is going on, there is another equally important bond that shouldn't be forgotten—the bond between the parents. It's easy for parents to forget about each other when a baby comes along. Until your baby arrived, the family meant the two of you. After the baby, it's all about the baby. Your relationship with your partner is going to change. That's a given. How can it be otherwise? Your role in life has changed from partners to parents. For most of you, parenthood becomes one of the major roles, if not *the* major role, of your life. Speaking as a pediatrician, I can't argue that this is a bad thing. But at the same time, it would be a shame if your relationship as a couple suffered as a result of your becoming parents. This doesn't have to be the case.

As corny as it sounds, you really ought to think about carving out at least a little time now and then dedicated only to each other, and not just in the bedroom (though I'm not discounting the bedroom). For parents, especially new parents, this means making a special effort and perhaps burning precious calories to spend time with each other, even if only in conversation.

Parents come to learn the value of what we call an "adult conversation," a *conversation with an adult*, preferably your partner. After talking to an infant all day, you will understand how restorative and satisfying adult conversation can be. Try it.

Reading Your Baby's Cues

In one sense, babies are easier to understand than adults. Unlike us, they haven't developed superegos and consciences. They don't know how to use guile or subterfuge. They don't lie. They don't even kid around. That's the good news. The bad news is that the signals the baby does communicate to us can be devilishly difficult to decode.

I remember our own first baby's pediatrician counseling us (yes, we take our child to a pediatrician who is not me). He told us, "The baby's signals will get easier to read with time." I was reassured to hear this. Unfortunately, he was wrong. I don't think I ever learned to read our first baby's cues. My wife was much more successful at this since she spent nearly 24 hours a day with our son for the first year of his life. It turns out that just spending time with a baby is the best way to learn to read her cues. For the rest of us, a quick study guide can help prepare you to become an expert cue-reader.

Visual Cues

You would think that visual cues would be easy to read. After all, you only have to look at your baby to get a sense of what's going on with her. But a newborn sleeps for about 20 hours per day! How do you read a sleeping baby? In fact, it's even tougher than this. Quietly sleeping babies often breathe so gently that you cannot even tell they are breathing.

Newborn babies have a peculiar breathing pattern. They go from imperceptible quiet breathing to deep and sometimes loud breathing, and back again. This unpredictable pattern can be disturbing for some new parents to observe, but it's quite normal. It's called *periodic breathing*, meaning that there's an ebb and flow, or periodicity, to the baby's breathing pattern. Like many infantile patterns, periodic breathing goes away after about two months.

Still, if you're like me, you worry when you see your baby sleeping quietly in the bassinet or Moses basket and you aren't sure if she's actually breathing. When my boys

What NOW?

What Does It Mean?

Some facial expressions have no meaning, but parents often misinterpret them. Many parents believe, for example, that a trembling lower lip means the baby is cold. In fact, this behavior has nothing to do with the temperature. Rather, it is yet another infantile reflex that the baby typically sheds by about two months of age.

Another expression that is often misinterpreted is lip-sucking or lip-smacking. Babies do this naturally all the time when they are not necessarily hungry. If the baby has just fed and burped and seems nice and contented but starts sucking at her lower lip, it does not always mean she's still hungry. It's just a reflex that the baby has not shed. On the other hand, if the baby wakes up after the normal interim between feedings and starts sucking her lip, she may actually be hungry. The key difference is the context. In the first case, she just ate, so the lip-sucking shouldn't be interpreted as a feeding cue. In the second case, when it's been a while since she's eaten and she's just starting to stir, it's time to feed her again.

were sleeping like this, I ever-so-gently "accidentally" nudged the bassinet—not so hard as to wake them up but hard enough to make them flinch or startle. Of course, it isn't necessary to do this, but as an experienced parent I can appreciate how reassuring it can be to verify that the baby is still breathing.

Baby expressions

Until your baby learns to smile reflexively, there are really only two expressions that provide clues to what she is feeling. The first is... well, *nothing*. Most content babies show no particular facial expression whatsoever. Keep in mind, however, that the expressionless baby is probably happy. At the very least she is not *unhappy*.

Pre-cry face pucker

The social or gas smile: Which is it?

But if your baby is uncomfortable, or wants something from you, her face will let you know. Babies can transition almost instantly from happy and contented to unhappy. You'll begin to see signs of the change around her mouth as the muscles begin to tighten and the mouth opens. Your baby will be only a few seconds away from crying.

The Gas Smile

Early on, while it's true that real baby smiles do occasionally sneak across a baby's face, more often than not an apparent smile probably is a "gas smile." It's not clear why babies do this. Sometimes it's hard to tell what's happiness and what's gas. I believe it's best to assume it's happiness and to smile right back at your baby.

The Happy Dance

When our elder son was eight weeks old, we noticed him behaving oddly. He appeared to be fascinated with the black-and-white mobile that we had suspended over his crib. He stared at the mobile and began to wave his arms and legs, alternating as though he were marching, staring straight at the mobile. At first we had no idea what he was doing. We found it amusing, though, and sometimes did his little dance alongside him.

A week or so later, when Noah developed his social smile, the mystery cleared up: As soon as he lay beneath his mobile, he broke out in a big, broad smile, then started the rhythmic, marching movements with his arms and legs. The little dance he was doing was his way of expressing his pleasure—though his face remained totally expressionless. His brain was registering happiness and his arms and legs were showing just how happy he was, but without the smile it was difficult to read what was going on.

Brazilians have a name for this phenomenon. They call it a *Dança da Felicidade*, The Happy Dance.

I Want; Therefore I Cry: Deciphering the Real "Baby Talk"

The auditory cue that may be the most difficult to interpret is the cry. Babies' needs are fairly straightforward so they cry for basically three reasons: because they're hungry, because they're uncomfortable, or because they just want to be held. The trick is to figure out what it is the baby wants. We'll deal with each cry separately.

The "I'm hungry!" cry

If the baby eats every two to three hours and it's time to eat, her crying could mean she's hungry. As we'll discuss in Chapter 4, you'll want to avoid delaying feeding to the point that the baby starts to cry. The "I'm hungry!" cry is fairly loud and insistent, often accompanied by rooting behavior. *Rooting* is the name for the baby's natural reflex to look around for a nipple somewhere near her face. The rooting expression appears as almost a half-smile. What's actually happening is the baby is opening her mouth in part to signal to you that she's hungry and in part hoping to hook a nipple in the vicinity.

After about a minute, the "I'm hungry!" cry can get louder, more insistent, and more piercing until it seems as though the baby is in pain. She's not in pain; she's just really upset because she's so hungry. And this creates a problem for her. When a baby is wailing because she's so upset about her hunger, she may be too upset to calm down, slow her breathing, put a nipple in her mouth, and start to feed, so it will be difficult to get her to stop crying.

When a baby is lost in the fog of her own hysterical crying, it's difficult but not impossible to find your way through to her. The first trick is to try to remain calm yourself. If the baby senses that you, too, are on the edge of tears (or perhaps crying yourself), she'll probably feel even more upset. Try to muster all your best acting ability and pretend you are calm, cool, and collected.

One method to get your baby to stop crying and to start feeding is to gently rock her while waiting for her to come down a bit from her hysterical peak or to wait for a pause in her wailing while she takes a breath. When this happens, try to introduce the nipple and see if she begins to suck and calm down.

Another method is to lay the baby on her back and place a thumb in each of the baby's palms. Then raise her hands up to her mouth, placing one of her hands against her lips. As she's rooting, she may start sucking her fingers and stop crying for a moment. Meanwhile, you'll want to bend over and bring your head close to hers. You can say "Shhhhhhhh" really calmly and serenely or you can just talk to your baby in a calm voice. You might notice her body begin to relax and her breathing begin to slow down. This is the time to put her to the breast or get that bottle in her mouth.

If none of these techniques work, it could be that your baby isn't hungry as much as she's uncomfortable.

The "Something's bothering me!" cry

This cry sounds a little harsher and more insistent than the "I'm hungry!" cry. It's worth mentioning here that even if your baby is uncomfortable for some reason, she might be comforted by feeding. But after a quick feed, you'll notice that your baby is still uncomfortable because she'll start crying again. Sometimes after a normal feeding, your baby will start crying because she has a gas bubble or because her wet or dirty diaper is bothering her. The solution in this case is not to try feeding her again; the solution is to try to find out what the problem is.

If your baby has just fed, or has fed recently, and you've determined that hunger is not the problem, there are a couple of places to look right away. First, has your baby pooped or peed recently? Many babies don't care at all if their diaper is wet or dirty, but some babies care a great deal. It's fairly easy and straightforward to undress your baby's bottom half and check the diaper. If it's dirty or wet, you can change it and see if this makes a difference to your baby.

Another likely source of discomfort for your baby is her stomach. Actually, the problem is rarely the stomach itself. It's either her intestines (large and small) or her esophagus (the tube between the mouth and the stomach).

When a baby's intestines get full of gas or poop, it can be painful, and she'll probably cry. There are many techniques available to you to try and relieve the baby's gas or other intestinal distress. I'll discuss many of them in Chapter 5. Sometimes just being with your baby and holding her while she deals with a gas bubble can help her feel better.

Many babies cry because they have reflux. The technical name for this kind of reflux is gastroesophageal reflux. Simply put, this is milk that starts in the stomach and moves backward, up into the esophagus instead of down into the intestines. I'll talk about reflux at length in Chapter 8.

Finally, some babies who cry have good, old-fashioned colic. I discuss the "C" word at greater length in Chapter 5.

The "Hold me!" cry

After hunger and discomfort, the most common reason a baby cries is that she just wants to be held. This cry is more of a whimpering, miserable cry. Babies seem to have an instinctive need to be held and comforted, especially by their mothers and fathers. Sometimes the need is greater than at other times. I suppose parents have the same needs with respect to holding their babies. Unfortunately, the deal seems to work out to the baby's advantage.

This is because your baby doesn't only want you to hold her—she also probably wants you to hold her while you're standing up. Hundreds of parents have told me how their babies seem to know that mom or dad sat down, because they start crying again. And it gets worse: They don't want you merely to stand with them, they want you to walk with them. This can seem very labor-intensive at 4:00 in the morning.

Can You Hold a Baby Too Much?

There's an old cultural myth that says if you hold an infant too much she'll become spoiled. All theories of parental-infant bonding reject this myth. In fact, most experts agree that for most of the first six months, the word "spoiled" doesn't even exist in the baby's "vocabulary." That is to say, it is impossible to spoil an infant by holding her too much. To the contrary: Prior to around four to six months of age, infants lack the internal means to soothe themselves. They require something (usually someone) outside themselves to feel calm and secure. This is a period of life when parents really have to respond when the baby cries. At the one-month well-baby visit, parents often ask me whether they can just let the baby cry. I usually respond, "Sure, you can... it won't work, though." Bottom line: Hold your baby as long as you want. You couldn't spoil her if you tried.

Genetics, Environment, and the Person Your Baby Will Become

One of the more common questions parents ask me is, "What color do you think her eyes will be?" It's a fairly simple question, with a not-so-simple answer. But for me, the question also peels back the cover from a much deeper philosophical question about the child's nature and the type of person she will become. I'll deal with the eye question first, though.

There are two groups of parents who never ask me about eye color: Scandinavians and African Americans. That is because they already know what color their baby's eyes are going to be. For everybody else, it's a toss-up. Eye color, like every other physical trait, is inherited from one's parents, but it's not a simple exercise to figure out what color a child's eyes are going to be. I have many blue-eyed children in my practice who have brown-eyed biological parents. Sometimes these children's grandparents have had blue eyes, but sometimes not. Eye color is inherited in what we call a *multifactorial way*; that is, many factors go into it in addition to the color of the parents' eyes.

This question becomes even more complicated because children's eye color tends to change with time. There's a lot of lore out there about the precise age at which one knows the final color of a child's eyes: four months, six months, two years, three years... but the truth is that it depends on the child.

Most babies' eyes start out a deep, cobalt blue, or "baby blue," because the iris (the colored part of the eye) is not fully developed, and the pigment cells that give rise to eye color have not fully formed at birth. As a result, eye color changes gradually over months, if not years, again depending on the child.

Eye color is a good metaphor for the development of the child in general. We never really know how a child is going to turn out. It's tempting to ask a pediatrician to predict many things about a child: How tall is she going to be? Can we tell how smart she's going to be? What color hair will she have? Will he go bald when he's older?

Hair color is sometimes easier to predict. The progression of a child's hair color often follows the pattern that a parent's hair color followed. For example, many parents tell me that they were towheaded until age seven when their hair started to turn brown. The same pattern often happens to their children's hair. But sometimes hair color ends up being something of a surprise, like eye color. It's best just to wait and see: Whatever color hair your child grows will be beautiful.

The heritability of intelligence is a controversial topic. The human ability to reason, to observe and draw inferences, to make connections and to draw distinc-

A Perfect Blend

A beautiful girl in my practice is the daughter of an African-American mother and a Scots-Irish father. When she was born, the girl had very light skin, like her father. Her mother has lovely dark skin and is justifiably proud of it. Mom was worried. "Is she going to stay this color?" she asked me. I knew that *melanin*, the substance that gives skin its darker tone, sometimes takes weeks to months to populate skin cells. "Just wait a little while," I reassured her, "She'll darken up." And she did. Today, the girl's skin tone is a gorgeous combination of her father's and her mother's skin tones.

tions—all are attributes that separate us from lower animals. When talking about human development, in general the rule is: the higher the function, the greater the range of normal. Like eye color, intelligence is multifactorial. That is to say, there are hundreds, possibly thousands, of factors that determine a child's intelligence, many of them genetic and many of them environmental. Determining how much heredity as opposed to a child's environment influences intelligence varies depending on how researchers perform their measurements. So smart parents tend to have smart kids, but it isn't entirely clear if it's the parents' genes that make the child smart or if it's the intellectually stimulating environments that smart parents provide.

There is one physical attribute that is much less genetic than people think, which is what we euphemistically refer to as "body habitus," or more precisely, how chubby your child is. When it comes to weight, genetics is not destiny. Just because a child's parents are heavy does not mean that the child will be heavy. To be sure, there are certain genetic factors that influence body weight, such as a tendency to low thyroid function, to name one. But *energy balance,* that is, the difference between what a person takes in and what the person expends in terms of calories, is independent of genetics—it's due entirely to diet and exercise. Healthy diet, exercise, and sleep aren't characteristics we are born with; they are habits we learn, mostly from parents.

Whatever color your child's eyes end up being, whatever the color of her hair, whatever her ultimate height and weight, and however smart she ends up being, one thing is certain: She will be unlike any human being who has ever lived on Earth, and there have been a lot of humans. I recommend thinking less about what her ultimate attributes will be. Instead, just stand back and marvel at your child's uniqueness. Harvard professor Michael Sandel calls this exercise "Openness to the Unbidden." That is to say, rather than focusing on what you want for intelligence, size, and eye color, simply watch in awe as this unique individual takes shape. This, of course, does not absolve you from the responsibility of taking care of her and teaching her right from wrong. It means only that regardless of how we try to mold our children according to our will, we always fail. At the end of the day we don't procreate; at best we *co*-create.

- How do you deal with grandma?
- How do you introduce your baby to her siblings, your pet, relatives, and close friends?
- How do you set limits on visitors?
- How do you negotiate the outside world with your baby, whether you're walking around the block or flying across the country?

Chapter 3

The World Beyond

To this point, I've discussed the things you can expect from your baby and how she interacts with you. Next, you and your baby are going to have to discover together how to negotiate the world beyond the nuclear family. That world beyond includes not only siblings but also grandparents, pets, friends of the family, and passersby in the street. There are a few simple recommendations on how to make the transition from couple-without-children to parents-of-their-very-own-baby.

This Is *YOUR* Baby!

Now that you've got your baby home and you've become acquainted, it's a good time to remind yourself of a simple but crucially important fact: This is *YOUR* baby!

By the time you've brought your baby home, you've probably been bombarded with advice about how to take care of her. Some of this advice you may have solicited, but the majority is probably unsolicited. Trying to catch all the advice being flung at you can seem overwhelming. Sometimes I feel that my job as a pediatrician is to help new parents filter these streams of information into groups: the probably true, the definitely *not* true, and the vast gray area in between. Often your gut reaction to these pieces of advice is the most valuable. As one of my pediatric heroes, Benjamin Spock, advised new mothers over 50 years ago, "Trust yourself, you know more than you think you do!"

Dealing with Grandma

But how do you deal with those pieces of advice that come from your own mother or your mother-in-law? These are special cases that need to be dealt with delicately and in more detail.

First, a word of sympathy for your mother: A grandmother can be an extremely valuable resource. After all, the fact that you survived to have your own baby proves that your mom knew at least a little (and more likely a great deal) about raising children. Grandma can be an enormous help to you, especially in the first weeks and months of life. If she's relatively healthy and spry, she can help you a *lot*.

Remember that she's been your mother for a long time. The only way she's known you has been as a mother. It's difficult, sometimes impossible, for mothers to relinquish the mother role. By this I mean it can be difficult for your mother to resist the temptation to be a mother to your baby. But she *must* relinquish that role because *you're* the mother. One approach is to gratefully thank your mother for all her good help and advice... and then go do what you wanted to do in the first place. It's generally not a good idea to engage your mother in arguments about how to raise your baby. The only way to grow into a confident and competent mother is to be given the opportunity to trust your own judgment, as Dr. Spock advised.

And all this goes double for mother-in-law.

Dealing with Your Mother-in-Law

Originally from Brazil, Simone and Anderson have lived in the United States since childhood. Anderson's biological mother lives in Brazil and visited the States for the first time when Maria Gabriella, the couple's first baby, was born. As soon as "Vovô" (Grandma) arrived, Simone knew she was in for some trouble.

Brazilians possess their own unique set of customs and beliefs regarding babies, just like Americans and virtually every other ethno-cultural community. For example, Brazilians tend to err on the side of overdressing babies. Although the baby was born in July, Grandma insisted on dressing Maria Gabriella in two layers of clothes. Of course, Simone wanted to dress the baby coolly, particularly on hot days. She didn't know how to address this issue with her mother-in-law, whom she didn't know very well, and Anderson was also reluctant to confront his own mother. After all, Grandma had raised five children by herself, and they all survived infancy!

I suggested to Simone that she transfer the decision-making responsibility to me. If there was ever a dispute between mom and mother-in-law, I suggested that Simone declare that Dr. Lindeman says (for example) the baby should only wear one layer of clothing, even if she hadn't actually spoken to me first! I'm happy to play the role of the "heavy" in disputes such as these if doing so helps maintain peace in the family.

Your Other First Baby: Introducing Your Newborn to Her Sibling(s)

As hard as you may try to prepare an older brother or sister for the arrival of your baby, the actual event almost always ends up being very different from what your older child (and you!) expected. Mom may have spent lots of time explaining to her child that "there's a baby in my belly," and that mommy will be going to the hospital to have the baby, and so on. But until the day arrives, these conversations are just stories that usually don't help a young child understand what is about to happen. When our second child was born, I thought I had a pretty good idea of what it was like to bring home a baby. In fact, I had no idea what it was like to have a toddler and a baby. Naturally, our two-and-a-half-year-old was even more clueless!

First, some good news: The meeting of your older child and your baby is going to go better than you think it will. There will certainly be moments when the older child will insist that you put your baby down. There may be regression, particularly of potty training (after all, the baby gets to wear a diaper, why can't I?). There may be acting out. All of this is normal. What the big sibling doesn't know is that this baby will one day worship the ground on which the big sibling walks!

Many parents arrange to have the baby "buy" a present for the older child. Sometimes the gift is presented at the same time the child comes to meet the baby. The mother and father can hand the gift to the new big brother and say, "Look what the baby got for you!" This often can soften the impact of the first meeting with the baby, which can sometimes be overwhelming for a small child.

Your Other, Other First Baby: Introducing Your Newborn to Your Pet(s)

If your life story is like that of many contemporary Americans, chances are you had a pet in your house long before you brought a baby home. Frequently your relationship with the pet dog or cat is as old as your relationship with your spouse, and in some cases it's older. This section deals with managing the transition from your pet being the "baby" in the house to being the big sibling, in a manner of speaking. The discussion focuses mostly on dogs and cats. Other domestic mammals such as rodents (guinea pigs, hamsters, rats), rabbits, ferrets, and such don't really notice anything is amiss in their world unless you neglect to feed them. Fish, reptiles, and amphibians couldn't care less. It's a placental-mammal thing: They wouldn't understand.

The scent

Your animal can't speak, but she isn't *that* dumb (this goes for you cat owners out there, too). She knew when you were pregnant that something was up. For one thing, you smelled different. Animals are scenting experts, and pets tend to be sensitive to nonverbal cues. If you and your spouse are excited or nervous about the prospect of having a baby, your animal notices.

Some dogs respond by acting out—being noisier and more demanding. Others get sulky. Other dogs don't seem to notice that mom's belly is four times larger than it was a few months ago. Cats continue to sniff their food, walk away, and curl up in a warm place.

Guess who's coming to visit... forever!

After the birth but before coming home from the hospital, many parents prepare their dog by bringing home a receiving blanket that the baby has slept in. The dog will know right away that you've been around another human, though of course she won't understand that mom has had a baby and that she's sleep deprived, struggling with nursing, and so on. There's only so much information a canine can assimilate.

When the baby comes home, it might be a good idea for you to have the baby "bring the dog a present," just as you would for a big sibling. For most dogs this is unnecessary. To the happy-go-lucky, well-adjusted dog, a new chewy toy is a just a new chewy toy. But for your more high-strung canines, a toy may be just the distraction she needs.

Enthusiasm

When you bring your baby home, your dog is likely to be excited to see you. After all, you've been gone for a few days. Take charge of larger animals that might jump up onto the tender uterus of the new mother. Cats will probably sniff the baby and the car seat and then slink away under the couch.

Many new parents are concerned that their dog will hurt their new baby. There's something important to realize about your dog: She is unlikely to hurt your new baby on purpose, but she can hurt your baby by accident. Puppies especially tend to bubble over with enthusiasm. In this respect they are a lot like toddlers. It is easier to teach puppies than older dogs, however, what is acceptable in the house and what is not. It's a curious fact of life that a dog is easier to train than a child. No wonder they are our best friends.

Unless your dog is older or extraordinarily well-behaved, it's probably a good idea to physically separate the baby area from the dog's domain. For many families the kitchen is the natural location for the dog. If you don't have a full kitchen, there are many other creative ways to divide the territory by using gates where possible or pieces of furniture if necessary.

When things go wrong...

Sadly, some dogs and cats just don't react well to the introduction of a new baby. Some dogs react by behaving inappropriately. Often these animals display their aggression at you, not at your baby. After all, you brought the baby home—she didn't bring herself! Some dogs only seem to get upset when their preferred "parent" holds the baby. Like many older siblings, the animal just needs some quality time of her own.

Some cats hide themselves away and refuse to eat for a period. In either case, the dark period is usually short-lived. In most cases, the animal accepts the baby as a *fait accompli* and gets on with her life.

MY baby!

Most dogs instinctively accept the baby into their family as if she were one of their own. This can be a wonderful and endearing quality of an animal... until guests come over. I once scheduled a home visit with a new baby whose family owned a large Doberman. The parents asked me to call when I neared the house since they had learned that their dog quickly became territorial when strangers came near the baby. They needed to move their dog into the garage prior to my arrival. I appreciated their thoughtfulness.

Where's That Baby? Dealing with Visitors

It's a fact of life: Folks are going to want to see your baby. Your friends and family are thrilled for you and they want to share your joy. Many people love seeing a newborn baby. If this is true for your close friends, it is no less true for people in your social circles such as houses of worship, clubs, and others.

There is nothing intrinsically wrong with people wanting to see your baby. It's just that you and your potential visitors should consider your needs and the needs of your baby as well. You're going to be tired. In fact, you're likely going to be profoundly sleep-deprived. I suggest to moms that they get as much sleep as they can. If this means sleeping during the day while the baby is sleeping, that's what the mom should do, but it's not practical to lie on the couch and take a nap while friends or family are over for a visit.

You should resist the temptation to act as hostess for your guests. Many moms I visit are vacuuming and even cooking with a newborn baby sleeping in a bassinet. Please let others clean and cook; you have your hands full with that baby. If guests want to come over to help you, that's wonderful. Many people will want to bring you baby gifts. That is why I recommend never buying clothes for your new baby. Your friends and family will take care of that for you. Really good friends will cook for you or bring food over. Some communities, religious and otherwise, organize committees to keep good food in new parents' home in the first few weeks of the baby's life. This is a great community-building activity, and it should be encouraged.

How many?

There's a reason hospitals limit the number of visitors you can have during visiting hours. Too many visitors place stresses and strains on your body. The stress can increase your postpartum pain and can even diminish or delay breast-milk production. Stress should be kept to a minimum and so should the number of visitors. One person at a time or one small family at a time is the maximum.

Just as small children tend to be bored in hospital rooms, they tend to be bored with baby visits. There's nothing to play with there. Actually it's worse than that: There *are* things to play with in hospital rooms—emergency buttons, the controls on your bed, even the volume control on your television—but a child really shouldn't play with them. In your house, there's probably plenty of stuff for a small child to play with, and much of it likely makes a lot of noise. If so, the amount of time the child stays should be kept to a minimum. Babies aren't really interesting to small children anyway.

Think of your home as a much more comfortable hospital room. Just as in the hospital, fewer visitors mean less stress for you and for your baby. Don't forget that all your baby's senses are working. She can hear the visitors even when she's asleep. And she can certainly feel the jostling from being picked up and passed around!

Many parents ask me how many hours per day guests should stay. The answer depends on how you're feeling. It also depends on what kind of day your baby is having. Has she been feeding and sleeping well? If the answer is no, it's probably a bad idea to make her day tougher by subjecting her to the additional stress of visitors. One hour is plenty of time for guests to see the baby, wish you well, perhaps put away some of your dishes, and say good-bye.

"I have a cold. I'll just kiss your cheek."

It's a difficult thing to ask ill friends and relatives to hold off on their visit until they're feeling better. Nevertheless, your baby's health—and yours—are much more important than their visit. Most of the illnesses we're worried about are viruses spread by contact. If a sick person comes to your house and touches a table, then you touch the table, then you touch your baby, it's as though the sick person has touched your baby. Sick people should delay their visit until they've recovered.

Even if family and friends are feeling fine, it's a good idea for everybody to wash their hands before touching the baby. Many families leave a big dispenser of hand sanitizer on a table near the baby. You needn't feel embarrassed about asking people to wash their hands. Tell them the doctor said so.

The key thing to remember regarding visitors is limiting stimulation. Keep in mind how your baby is like a pinball machine: Less stimulation is better than more. Even though you have guests, it's a good idea to keep the lights low and for everybody to sit, relax, and speak quietly. In general, I prefer that as few people as possible pick up the baby, particularly if she's sleeping.

Steppin' Out with My Baby

I get a ton of questions from new parents about leaving the house with a new baby. Unfortunately, there's a lot of mythology about the outside world and babies. Many people believe that evil humors float on the air outside that could harm a baby. Others believe that air and wind are bad for a baby. The truth about the outside is that it depends on the weather, the time of year, and the temperature.

What to Take Along When You Leave Home

- A change of clothes and plenty of diapers and accessories. Because stuff happens.

- Hand sanitizer for strangers who insist on touching your baby but also for general cleanups.

- A covering for the stroller to keep out the sun.

- Bottles ready to go or a way to cover yourself if you need to breast-feed. Many communities welcome breast-feeding mothers in public, but some do not. If you find yourself in a place with a hungry baby, if possible check ahead of time if the place where you are is okay for public breast-feeding. When in doubt, err on the side of discretion.

Dressing

The rule of thumb for dressing a baby for leaving the house is that your baby should wear one more layer of clothing than you would wear leaving the house. The exception is a hat. Even if you aren't in the habit of wearing a hat, your baby should wear one. Keep in mind that babies have relatively large heads compared to the rest of their bodies, and a lot of heat escapes from that location.

If you are uncomfortable with the temperature when you step outside, whether it's cold or hot, you can be sure that your baby will be uncomfortable, too. On days like these, I don't recommend going outside unless you absolutely have to, and then for as briefly as possible—for instance, to a preheated car.

Parents also want to know what to do about taking a baby outside in the summer on a really hot, sunny day. We don't recommend sunscreen on babies until they are at least six months old, so keep your baby out of direct sunlight. This may mean long cotton sleeves, a hat for your baby, and especially some kind of sun shield or drape over the baby carrier.

It's especially important to keep sun out of your baby's eyes. Most babies are unable to keep sunglasses on because they don't have a well-developed nose bridge. Many babies also object to the feeling of something wrapped around their eyes so they try to remove it! Make sure your baby's hat has a big enough brim to shade the eyes, or that the whole baby stays in the shade.

Sometimes the weather is just so beautiful it would be a shame *not* to take the baby out for a walk. Fresh air really is as good for you as your parents said it is so a walk would be good for you and your baby. Most babies find the low-frequency gentle rumble of wheels on the pavement soothing, sort of like a white-noise machine. Other parents like to walk with the baby strapped to them or hung in a sling. Either way can be enormously enjoyable for you and your baby.

What do you do about people on the street who want to "see" your baby? (In our society, "seeing" often means "touching.") Everybody wants to touch your baby. Of course, you don't want to seem rude by saying no. But just as in your house, people on the street shouldn't touch your baby unless they've washed their hands. Many people hang a small container of hand sanitizer on the stroller or car seat for this purpose, but sometimes it's just easier to tell a little white lie. I give my new parents permission to tell people on the street that the doctor says people aren't allowed to touch the baby. I don't mind being the bad guy for the sake of a new baby.

Taking the Show on the Road: Traveling with Your Baby

Parents frequently ask me if it's okay to take their baby travelling, and if so, when? Often they have planned the trip prior to their baby's arrival. Sometimes there are family members who live far away who would love to see the baby. For some, emailed photos and even videoconferencing software are poor substitutes for seeing the baby in person.

When can I travel?

The first question is always, "When can I travel with my baby?" The short answer is another question: When are you leaving the hospital? That is to say, in cases of emergency, when you absolutely must leave as soon as possible, you can literally leave the hospital and head for the airport. There are certain things you need to know about such travel that I'll deal with later.

The long answer is also another question: Why do you want or need to travel? If the trip is not urgent, you might consider waiting until you and your baby have a routine down, especially for feeding (so that you can mess up your routine by travelling).

But seriously, there will not be a better age to travel with your baby than during her first year. As long as all you have to do is stop to feed and change your baby, travel is relatively easy. Travelling with a toddler or older child is far more difficult for reasons that will become obvious once you try it.

The vaccination status of your baby doesn't really matter that much. Therefore, it's not necessary to wait until your baby has had her first or her second set of vaccines. I do recommend, however, that you plan your trip so that your baby will not miss vaccination visits. These are typically done at two, four, and six months of age. Catching up becomes tricky at these early ages if you miss vaccine visits.

Travel by air

During the first six months, you won't have to purchase a ticket for your baby. She'll sit in your lap. Airlines understand this. They've flown thousands of babies before. You'll want to transport your baby around the airport in a car seat, so you'll probably have to check this item at the gate.

There are a few crucially important things to keep in mind about air travel. Most parents are concerned about their baby's ears on takeoff and landing. I'm really not concerned at all. You can nurse or give a bottle during takeoff and landing to allow your baby to equalize the pressure behind her eardrums, but this is not necessary. What *is* necessary is infection control.

Airports and airplanes are essentially contaminated places. Think about this: Thousands of people pass through airports and hundreds ride on the same airplane every day. Significant numbers of travelers are ill with some kind of virus that they carry on their hands. The sick travelers frequently touch places such as the ticket counter or the armrests in the waiting areas. When you then touch these places and touch your baby, you pick up the sick person's viruses and pass them on to your baby.

The "toucher" and the "baby-holder"

If you are travelling with someone in addition to your baby, I recommend that you designate a "toucher." The toucher is the person who is assigned to touching all the potentially contaminated surfaces: the ticket counter, the handrails, and the heavy bags, for example. The person on baby duty, usually the mother, should hold the baby. The baby-holder should try strenuously to avoid touching anything that she doesn't absolutely have to touch.

I recommend bringing along plenty of hand sanitizer and baby wipes. Both the designated toucher and the baby-holder should use lots of both frequently. The rules set down by the Transportation Safety Administration (TSA) are more or less stringently enforced depending on the airport and the destination. To err on the side of safety, carry the hand sanitizer and the wipes in a transparent one-quart Ziploc bag so that the TSA screener can easily see what you're carrying. It's always a good idea to call the airline ahead of time and ask if there will be restrictions on the size of the hand sanitizer container.

Speaking of the TSA and scanners, any item that you can feed the baby or place on her skin can go through an X-ray machine without damaging it. This includes frozen breast milk. The baby herself should probably not pass through an X-ray screener if at all possible. The small amount of radiation delivered is not harmful; it is simply unnecessary.

If you are flying across time zones, keep in mind that your baby will likely behave as though she is in the time zone you left for longer than you will. This jet lag tends to disrupt sleep and eating schedules, but your baby will quickly recover upon returning home.

Miles to go before I sleep: Travel by car

Long-distance travel by car is exactly like short-distance travel by car. The only difference is that you have to stop frequently to change and feed your baby. If you have a big enough car, you can change your baby in the back seat. If this proves too difficult, most public bathrooms (even men's rooms!) come equipped with changing tables.

Your baby is likely to sleep for much of even a fairly long trip. This is because the car acts as a large six-cylinder white-noise machine, which tends to induce sleep. This is all well and good while you are actually travelling, but once you reach your destination your baby's disrupted sleep pattern may come back to bite you in the form of nighttime sleeplessness and difficulty feeding. This effect may be minimized by frequent stops for feeding that mimic as closely as possible the baby's usual feeding pattern.

Trains and boats

Trains and boats are fantastic ways to travel with a baby. You are afforded all the conveniences of air travel without being confined to too-small a seat and difficult access to the bathroom. You can feed your baby on a more natural schedule and sleep far more comfortably than in the car. And babies don't get seasick.

Breast-feeding on the road

Nursing shawls offer a discreet solution to nursing in public, where appropriate. You can watch your baby while she feeds.

The world is not yet a 100% breast-feeding-friendly place. You never can tell if you are in a location where public breast-feeding is commonly accepted. To err on the safe side and to respect the sensibilities of your hosts on the road, it's best to acquire a breast-feeding hood that allows you to feed your baby discreetly in public. The worst that could happen is that you might feel compelled to find a private room where you can be alone with your baby.

Contact!

Finally, keep in mind the rules of thumb for leaving the house with your baby. What holds true for the street where you live is true for strange cities: Folks should ask you before touching your baby and probably shouldn't do so unless they wash their hands first. This is where the travel hand sanitizer comes in handy. And of course, the stranger who has just sneezed into her hand should just keep walking rather than stop to ooh and aah over your baby.

Notes:

Chapter Highlights

- What are the basics of breast-feeding?
- What are the basics of bottle-feeding?
- What about the other end?
- When should I introduce solid foods?
- How do I troubleshoot feeding problems?

Chapter 4

Feeding Your Baby

Since this book deals with the first six months of a baby's life, the question of what to feed your baby has a fairly straightforward answer: milk! All a baby needs for the first six months of life is 20-calorie-per-ounce breast milk or infant formula. Of course, the topic gets a little more complicated because for a long time parents have been starting solids prior to six months. I'll talk about the subject of starting solids later in this chapter. For now, let's delve a little deeper into what an infant needs and how to give it to her.

Eating Well Is the Best Indicator of a Healthy Baby

At every well visit, regardless of a child's age, regardless of her medical history, and regardless of her weight percentile, I always talk about healthy eating. For a baby the discussion is easy because she is eating essentially one thing: milk. If the baby eats well and grows, it's nearly certain that the baby is healthy. Even babies who grow slowly may be perfectly healthy. Weighing and measuring may be the most important thing that I do every day to verify that a baby is growing well and getting enough nutrition. For babies who are breast-fed, weighing is the most accurate way to assess adequate nutrition since it's difficult or impossible to know how much milk these babies are taking in. This is one reason why there are so many visits to the pediatrician during the first year of a baby's life.

How Much and How Often to Feed

While you're still in the hospital with your baby, you may get lots of advice from many nurses, doctors, and consultants about how much and how often to feed her. Because there are a multitude of right ways to feed a baby and very few wrong ways, every piece of advice is at least slightly different from the others, and every piece of it is true. Here are a few rough guidelines.

If you're going to at least attempt breast-feeding, the recommendations about feeding are different for the days before breast milk comes in than after it comes in. There are a couple of important things to keep in mind while you're trying to get breast-feeding going.

The three thoughts

Three thoughts almost always enter the heads of new breast-feeding moms during the first few days of a baby's life. The first thought is, "I'm not making enough milk for her!" Fortunately, this is not true. A new mom *is* making enough milk for whatever day of life the baby's on. The first milk is called *colostrum*, sometimes referred to as "liquid gold" because of its value to the baby. Some women start making colostrum in the late stages of pregnancy. Most often, colostrum starts coming in on the day of birth or the day after.

Colostrum is more concentrated than the milk that will come in later, and it is darker yellow in color. This first milk is relatively rich in protein but has less fat and fewer carbohydrates than later milk. The reason is that these proteins help provide immunity (called "passive immunity" because the baby doesn't make the immune factors herself) and help stimulate development of the baby's intestines. So colostrum not only feeds the baby but also helps protect her from germs and speed the process of development. I usually recommend to new mothers that if they don't want to breast-feed, they should at least give the baby colostrum for a few days after birth. The health benefits to the baby can be enormous. And you can be sure that you're making enough milk for your baby. You're making more than it feels like you're making!

The second thought is, "My baby is starving!" Fortunately, this is also not true. Your baby is not starving, but it's understandable why you might think that way. About 24 hours after being born, a baby sort of "wakes up" and says, "You mean this isn't going to happen automatically? I have to feed myself?" Whereupon the baby begins sucking like mad, crying and fussing, and then goes back to more sucking like mad.

The truth is that the baby is not sucking like mad because she's starving. This intense sucking is what I refer to as "purpose-nursing." That is to say, she's nursing with a purpose, though she of course is not aware of what that purpose is. The purpose is to stimulate the process of making breast milk.

From time to time there is a third thought that enters a new mom's mind, which is, "Is my baby latching on properly?" There are a couple signs to look for.

- *Wider is better:* Try to get the baby to open her mouth as wide as possible before bringing her to the breast. Ideally, her tongue, bottom lip, and chin should touch the breast first, as far from the base of the nipple as possible.

- *Getting right to it:* If your baby starts sucking and swallowing right away, she probably has a good latch. You'll notice that she'll start with a few short quick swallows and then longer, deeper sucking. If she takes a few brief sucks and then falls asleep, she's probably not latched on.

- *Pain:* If it hurts when your baby is nursing, it may be that she hasn't latched on properly. Simply insert a finger in your baby's mouth to break the suction and start again.

Getting your baby to latch on

Learning how to help your baby latch on to the breast will make it easier for your baby to nurse and minimize sore nipples. From WomensHealth.gov.

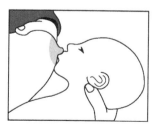 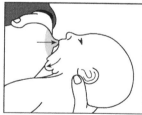 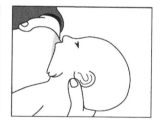

Tickle the baby's lips to encourage her to open wide.

Pull your baby close so that the chin and lower jaw moves into your breast first.

Watch the lower lip and aim it as far from the base of nipple as possible, so the baby takes a large mouthful of breast.

Breast-Feeding and Survival

Since breast-feeding is so difficult in the first few days of life, many mothers ask why breast milk isn't going full-blast when the baby is born. Why doesn't the system turn on some time during the last trimester so that we don't have to go through this stressful struggle? There is an answer to this question, and it is rooted in the origins of early humans.

There was a time in the not-so-distant past when human life was, in Thomas Hobbes' memorable phrase, "solitary, poor, nasty, brutish, and short." For prehistoric humans every meal was a challenge, and, more often than not, there were no meals. Under such circumstances, the chances that a baby would survive her first day of life were small. Pregnancy was dangerous, childbirth was potentially deadly, and nursing a newborn was fraught with danger for both mother *and* baby. A mother needs to consume about 500 calories per day over and above what she needs for her own survival to produce breast milk for her baby. The last thing she needed was to expend precious calories on a baby who didn't live past her first day.

So humans evolved (or were created with, if you prefer) a clever mechanism to protect the mother from compromising her own survival. If the baby was born sick or otherwise unable to survive, the mother didn't "waste" calories and risk starving herself. If, however, the mother gave birth to a big, vigorous baby, this usually meant that mother and baby were healthy and that the baby would survive. The baby rooted and sucked and cried loudly as if to say, "Here I am. Ya gotta feed me now!" The baby then sucked like mad for a couple of days and stimulated the process of making breast milk for herself.

Now fast-forward to the present. Most mothers in the U.S. today are healthy, well nourished, and well cared for throughout pregnancy and tend to give birth to healthy, vigorous, and *hungry* babies. Unlike in the old days, virtually all these babies survive. But our bodies have not caught up with our prosperity. New mothers continue to make breast milk the same way they did in prehistoric times, so it is easy for mothers today to conclude that something is wrong because at first they aren't making much milk.

Babies lose weight during the first few days of life. This is also part of the plan. They are born with a little extra weight to sustain them while baby and mom work on producing breast milk. This is also true for small full-term babies. Typically, a first-time nursing mom requires two weeks to get her baby back to birth weight. In my experience, however, it takes less time than this. Our first child was already above his birth weight before leaving the hospital.

These mothers need to know that there is nothing wrong. In fact, there's something right going on: They are walking along the same path as mothers have since the dawn of time.

When Milk Comes In

How quickly milk comes in depends on a number of factors, but it generally takes two to four days. One of the only advantages that a mother who has had a Cesarean section has over those who give birth vaginally is that she will still be in the hospital when her milk comes in. Most mothers who've had normal deliveries go home from the hospital *before* their milk has come in. For many of these mothers a lactation consultant can be a valuable source of comfort as well as information in the initial stages of breast-feeding. Maternity nursing staff in hospitals can help new moms locate lactation consultants. Your pediatrician can help you as well.

As a man, I can't describe for you what it feels like to have your breast milk come in. All I can report is what the mothers tell me. And most tell me that when it happens, *you know it.* It often starts with a tingling sensation around the armpits, then proceeds to a feeling of fullness and heaviness of the breasts that will be noticeable in the mirror. And the breasts may *hurt.* Some mothers with larger breasts might not notice changes themselves, but all mothers will notice changes in the way the baby eats.

Although in the first few days, mom feels as if she's not making enough milk, it quickly becomes the opposite: Mom is making *too much* milk! Unlike the perceived dearth of milk during the first couple days of a baby's life, however, this oversupply is often all too real. Some mothers' nipples may become flattened from the pressure of engorged breasts, making it difficult for the baby to latch on. For a mother's comfort, in addition to the benefit of the baby trying to get a latch, she may need to express some milk manually or with a pump. I caution mothers not to overdo any prefeeding milk expression, since the last thing they want to do is to overstimulate their breasts to make more milk than the baby wants. Another thing to keep in mind is that a mother's breasts may leak milk for a period of time, especially when the baby cries. This is the "let-down reflex." It is involuntary—something that you have no control over. It may be a good idea to buy some disposable nursing pads to avoid needing to change shirts several times a day.

Once milk comes in, babies gulp more than they suck. A mother will be able to hear her baby swallowing. Sometimes milk will dribble out of the side of the baby's mouth. But the most positive and satisfying sign that milk has come in is that the baby will appear more satisfied and sleep for longer between feedings. Often the baby will "pass out" in a "milk coma" after five minutes because of the sheer pleasure of having a stomach full of mother's milk.

From this point on, purpose-nursing is over and it's on to feeding on demand. Just as with babies who bottle-feed, feeding on demand means you feed your baby when she's hungry and *don't* feed her when she's not hungry. For breast-fed babies, this means 5 to 20 minutes per side every two to three hours. For bottle-fed babies, the amount a baby takes depends on her age. For the first few days, she'll take a half-ounce to an ounce every two to three hours. Shortly thereafter it will increase to one to two ounces every two to three hours.

Some babies take more than the average and some take less. Some feed more often and some feed less often. Breast-fed babies tend to nurse more often than bottle-fed babies in the first few days of life. After that, breast-fed and bottle-fed babies feed equally often, on average. If the baby is peeing and pooping a lot, and if she falls asleep after feeding, you can tell that the baby is probably taking what she needs. A normal breast-fed baby may poop every time you feed her. You may even notice the baby getting slightly bigger every day.

By the end of the first month, your baby will be taking about four ounces every two to four hours. This goes for breast-fed and bottle-fed babies alike. In case you are wondering if your baby truly is eating enough (especially breast-feeding moms), you'll probably have a weigh-in scheduled at the pediatrician's office around this time, just to verify that your baby is getting enough.

From one to six months your baby will take somewhere in the vicinity of 24 ounces per day. As with all matters having to do with feeding, some babies will take more and some will take less.

Benefits of Breast-Feeding for Your Baby

There are few things in life other than mother's milk about which I can say that a little is better than nothing. If a mother is at all able she should try to give her baby at least some colostrum, even if she doesn't plan to breast-feed. A little liquid gold is better than none.

Some argue that formula is easier to give to babies than breast milk, but I believe it's actually the other way around. The preparation time is zero. The temperature is always just right and never needs to be adjusted. You never need to worry about how much breast milk to prepare. This is because breast-feeding is a demand-driven process. That is to say, however much your baby demands in terms of length and frequency of feeding determines the amount of milk her mother will produce for the next feeding. Breast milk is also easier to digest than cow's-milk-based formula. And, it should be mentioned, breast milk is *free*.

Many other health benefits accrue to babies who are breast-fed, including correct jaw development, fewer dental caries, and fewer allergies. It also turns out that breast-fed babies get sick less often than bottle-fed babies, although the reasons for this are complex. It's probably a combination of the health benefits of breast milk and the fact that, because the baby is close to mom most of the day and not in a daycare center, she's not exposed to numerous respiratory and gastrointestinal viruses.

Breast-feeding also enhances babies' psychological development. In Chapter 2 where we discussed attachment between mother and baby, I underscored the importance of time spent with the baby face to face. The body contact that nursing entails also enhances maternal-infant attachment.

Benefits for the mother

The science of maternal responses to breast-feeding has turned up many surprising benefits. During breast-feeding, the mother's body releases hormones into her bloodstream, particularly oxytocin. It's known that oxytocin is beneficial to a new mother in the first day or two after birth because it encourages her uterus to contract to its original size and shape. Although this process can be slightly painful or uncomfortable for moms in the initial stages, the contraction of the uterus can help prevent dangerous postpartum hemorrhages. That is why some women receive artificial oxytocin intravenously after they give birth. Oxytocin also tends to calm a woman's brain and make her feel more at ease with her baby. As I mentioned in Chapter 2, the attentive baby will absorb her mother's calm demeanor.

It also turns out that breast-feeding moms lose their "baby weight" faster. This is partially due to the extra calorie requirements imposed on their bodies by breast-milk production. There may also be a simultaneous increase in the rate of a mother's metabolism while breast-feeding. Longer-term health benefits have been shown to be associated with breast-feeding as well, including reductions in the incidence of type 2 diabetes, breast cancer, ovarian cancer, and postpartum depression.

Benefits for the rest of us

You may not appreciate that your decision to breast-feed your baby benefits others outside your family, but it does. Averaged over an entire population, it turns out that breast-fed babies get sick less often than bottle-fed babies, providing a cost savings to parents, their employers, and to the health care system as a whole. If you're breast-feeding, it means you aren't contributing to the pile of plastic, rubber, and paper trash that is generated from bottle-feeding. So breast-feeding is better for the environment as well.

Bottle-feeding is okay, too

Some women can't breast-feed because of medical reasons, and others choose not to breast-feed for any of a number of reasons. If you can't breast-feed or choose not to, you should know that you aren't harming your baby. Formula isn't poison, so you shouldn't be made to feel like a bad mother for bottle-feeding your baby. Some may criticize you or otherwise look cross-eyed at you, but they aren't the mother of your baby—you are! Sadly, there are many topics in child-rearing about which strangers on the playground claim to be expert. Even doctors who care for you and your baby may apply pressure, subtle or overt, regarding breast-feeding. You should know that they only have your best interests and the best interests of your baby in mind. But their advice should not be construed as criticism.

Formula Basics

Formulas are sold as ready-to-feed, concentrated, or powder. Ready-to-feed is the type you may see in the hospital in two-ounce bottles. This type tends to be substantially more expensive than powdered formula. Powdered formulas, sold in cans, are all formulated so that one level scoop of powder is added to two ounces of water.

You should use filtered water. It certainly does not need to be boiled unless it is drawn from a well. In general, if your water supply is derived from wells, it's best to use bottled water. For most communities, filtered water from the tap will do fine. The water should be warm but not hot. The classic method to test temperature is to run the water over your wrist. The skin on your wrist can accurately discriminate warm from hot water. Older infants don't seem to care if the water is room temperature or warm, so many parents prepare formula in room-temperature water.

Some parents prepare the formula and then heat the bottle. Do this carefully, inverting the bottle several times before testing the temperature (again on the wrist). Avoid heating infant formula in a microwave oven because microwaving creates hot spots in the bottle that can burn your baby's mouth.

Many parents add powder to water and shake the bottle vigorously. Doing this, however, introduces a fair amount of dissolved gas into the bottle that the baby then swallows, giving her worse gas than she might have otherwise. To allow the gas bubbles to rise to the top, set shaken bottles upright on the table for several minutes before serving, if the baby can stand the wait. Ideally, powdered formula should be swirled to mix, not shaken, to minimize bubble formation.

The bottle and the nipple

I get a lot of questions about bottles. What's the best kind of bottle to use? What kind of bottle is best for a colicky baby? What kind is the easiest or most convenient to use? In turn, I ask: Have you ever noticed that there are about fifty different kinds of bottles out there? If there were one kind of bottle that were superior to all the others, that's the only kind of bottle you'd have to buy. Rather than run down the list of the different types of bottles available, I'll only comment that if the first bottle you try doesn't seem like a good fit for your baby, keep trying different types until you hit on a design that your baby seems to like.

Nipple size

There are various nipple sizes, starting with the smallest, size 0, which is usually available only in hospitals for premature babies. The most common commercially available smallest nipple is size 1. Milk flows more slowly out of smaller nipple sizes and more quickly out of larger sizes. You can get a sense of the flow rate by turning a filled bottle upside down and observing milk drip out. Ideally it should not pour out, just drip. Some nipples also come marked with suggested ages for use. Like clothing sizes, you can be sure there is likely no correspondence between the suggested age for the nipple size and your baby's age.

The real test of flow rate happens when the baby drinks from the bottle. If the flow is too slow for her, she'll tug so hard at it that often she'll get frustrated and cry. If the flow is too fast, it can flood the baby's mouth and she might gag on the milk. (The same thing happens with an over-vigorous let-down reflex in a nursing mother.)

Do bottles have to be sterilized?

There's a lot of confusion about sterility. Bottles and nipples don't have to be boiled or run through a fancy machine to be sterilized (that is, made free of bacteria and viruses). A thorough washing with soap and hot water and good rinsing will remove all the germs. You then place the items on a rack and let them dry thoroughly. And you can trust your nose: If the bottles or the nipples don't smell right to you after thoroughly drying, throw them out.

BPA

There has been a lot of press in recent years about a substance present in plastic bottles called bisphenol-A (BPA). Researchers have discovered that small amounts of BPA can leach out of plastic bottles and even food can liners into food. There have been reports that BPA has been associated with various negative health effects, though no definitive link has been shown. Nevertheless, plastic bottle makers in the United States have begun producing bottles without BPA added. The BPA controversy turned many parent-consumers back to glass bottles. Glass bottles are great, but they break if you drop them. That's not good if there's a baby crawling around on the floor.

Types of formula

Formulas generally come in three "flavors": milk-based, soy-based, and elemental. The major difference between milk-based and soy-based formulas is the source of protein. Elemental formulas are predigested and consist of amino acids instead of entire proteins.

There are variations on all of these formulas. Some formulas are marketed as being better suited for fussy or colicky babies. Some of these formulas contain partially digested protein or only one type of milk protein. For babies who get fussy and don't seem to tolerate standard formula, it might be a good idea to try an "anti-colic" formula. You certainly should try these before making a bigger switch to soy-based formula (more on this later).

Some formulas contain less of the milk sugar *lactose*. Some are lactose-free. These formulas are good if your baby is recovering from a stomach bug. Normal full-term babies and babies who have recovered fully from stomach viruses have no need for lactose-free or lactose-reduced formulas because lactose intolerance is virtually non-existent in babies. I should emphasize here that lactose intolerance and milk-protein intolerance are separate entities. To understand them you only need to know the difference between lactose (sugar) intolerance and protein (milk-protein) intolerance. Nevertheless, a fair amount of confusion surrounds the two problems. The best thing that can be said about milk-protein intolerance and lactose intolerance in babies is that both are temporary. Your pediatrician can help you sort through the various approaches to choosing formula.

Organic vs. nonorganic

I have nothing against nonorganic formula. I have nothing against organic formula either. The truth is that organic formulas are no better than nonorganic formulas. As long as the prices of each brand are comparable it doesn't matter which you choose.

The goal in bottle-feeding is to get your baby to feed nearly silently; sucking noises probably mean she is taking in air. If you hold your baby at a 45-degree angle and hold the bottle at an angle so there is always formula in the neck and nipple, you should avoid gassy feeding.

On the subject of prices, here's a good word for the big-box stores: Buy in bulk, just as with diapers. It'll save you a ton of money over the long haul. You might even consider no-name brands. "Under the hood" they are almost indistinguishable from some major name-brand formulas.

How to prepare formula

I usually recommend preparing formula in two-ounce amounts. This is because it takes a single scoop of powder to prepare two ounces of formula. Of course, babies don't drink in two-ounce increments. If your baby drinks three ounces, I recommend making four ounces and discarding the fourth ounce if the baby doesn't drink it. Some people suggest putting the fourth ounce in the refrigerator and mixing it with new formula you make prior to the next feeding. In practice, this gets complicated, especially if you have to add half-scoops to water. If you do decide to save formula this way, just make sure you use the extra formula at the next feeding.

How to bottle-feed your baby

When giving the bottle you'll want to make sure your baby is swallowing formula, not air. One way to ensure that your baby is not gulping too much air is to hold her up at a 45-degree angle. Keep an eye on the formula in the bottle so that the level of the milk is above the nipple level. At the end of the bottle, your baby will swallow a fair amount of air. You'll want to make sure you get a good burp. If your baby has a tendency to swallow air or to be gassy, try to get a burp at the halfway point in the feeding as well.

No matter how you feed your baby, you will need to burp her. Hold the baby sitting on your lap, over your shoulder, or tummy down on your thighs, and gently pat the back until you hear a satisfying burp! Don't forget to use a towel or diaper to protect your clothes.

Switching formulas

When a baby seems uncommonly fussy or gassy on a formula, families often ask me about switching formulas. I like to answer, "Don't do it." Even though it may be the case that your baby isn't adjusting well to formula, in my experience, multiple formula switches seldom solve the problem. I like to talk to parents first about what the baby's symptoms are. It could be that the problem is reflux (see Chapter 8) or a more serious issue like a protein allergy (see below).

If a baby seems gassier than other babies or seems uncommonly fussy or colicky, I sometimes suggest a switch to a milk-based formula with semidigested protein or to a whey-only formula. I usually don't recommend a switch to soy-based formula unless it's pretty clear that the baby is allergic to milk protein. In general, avoid switching to soy without consulting your pediatrician, because soy-formula-fed babies make terrible-smelling poop. Lactose-reduced or lactose-free formulas are only useful if the baby has had a stomach bug. Otherwise they are gimmicks.

If the easy-to-digest formulas don't solve your baby's feeding problem, or if it's becoming clearer that the baby has an allergy to milk protein, then soy formula would be the next step.

The 48-Hour Rule

A Tip from Dr Rob:

Any time you switch formulas, I suggest sticking with the new option for longer than two days. This is because of the peculiar fact in pediatrics (perhaps in medicine in general) that everything seems to work for two days. If after 48 hours you are still getting the desired effect (happy, non-colicky baby), then you probably really *are* getting the desired effect, and you've made a successful switch.

If you've done a fair trial of both milk-based and soy-based formulas and the problem hasn't been solved, you might want to consult with your pediatrician. If you and the pediatrician are sure cow's milk and soy aren't working and if you've tried to treat your baby's reflux, then it may be time to switch to an elemental formula.

Elemental formulas are so named because the proteins and carbohydrates are broken down into smaller, easier-to-digest pieces. They are not broken down into actual elements, like carbon, oxygen, and hydrogen—although I cannot imagine formula made of elemental carbon tasting any worse than these formulas taste! Why babies like them remains a mystery to me.

Most babies with formula intolerance do well on elemental formulas. The problem with them is that they tend to be expensive. In my practice I have the parents buy the first can themselves. If the baby really takes to the formula, I write a prescription for the formula and send a prior authorization to the baby's insurance carrier with documentation that the baby has had bad reactions to both cow's-milk formulas and soy formulas. This can end up saving families a ton of money.

How Long Should I Breast-Feed or Bottle-Feed My Baby?

If you're talking about formula, the answer is easy: one year. A baby doesn't need formula beyond one year. You will find formulas on the shelf that are marketed for babies beyond the first year of life. Pay attention to the word "marketed." Formula companies have to make a buck like the rest of us, and I don't begrudge them that. But "toddler formulas" are gimmicks and you should avoid them. Your toddler won't need them. If your child is two weeks away from turning one and you run out of formula, switching to milk will not harm her. Similarly, if you have formula left over at your child's first birthday party, there's no reason to waste it. I tell parents there's nothing magical about the one-year mark. It's only the time it takes Earth to go around the sun once (and even that's off by about six hours).

If you are talking about breast-feeding, my answer is another question: How long do you want to keep it up? Here is the longer, more serious answer. I firmly believe that a little bit of breast-feeding is better than none, but the truth is that more is better by any measurement. It's better for the baby and it's better for the mother. But there is a point at which the nature of the benefits begins to change.

By about one year of age the relative importance of breast milk to a toddler's overall nutrition is much different from when the child is less than six months old. At the 12-month point the balance tips: Nursing is more beneficial in terms of comfort than nutrition. I have nothing against comfort. To the contrary: I only counsel mothers to understand the true benefit of breast-feeding beyond one year.

One bad reason to keep breast-feeding is the mistaken belief that it's a foolproof method of birth control. Breast-feeding is a lousy way to practice birth control. I've seen more mothers than I can count become pregnant while nursing.

I don't recommend breast-feeding older children because it often causes arguments. I counsel parents that if a mother engages in a verbal battle with her child about breast-feeding, it's probably time to call it quits. There are far too many battles over control and autonomy to fight during childhood. This is one that a mother needn't have with an articulate preschooler.

Some mothers choose to breast-feed two children simultaneously, their toddler and their newborn. I don't recommend this. As little as the toddler takes, she is taking milk away from her baby sister. Simultaneous nursing may also generate developmental regression, not to mention intense sibling rivalry. It's best to have number one weaned well before number two arrives.

But I'm going back to work

Work and breast-feeding *are* compatible! I know hundreds of mothers who have successfully breast-fed for several months after returning to work. You needn't think about weaning just because your medical leave is up. What might change is the proportion of breast-milk versus formula that your baby receives. This might happen because as your baby grows you might not be able to keep enough milk pumped and stored to sustain her while you're at work. This is not a problem: Most babies will not mind switching back and forth between breast milk and formula. In fact, most will gratefully accept whatever you give them.

The key will be deciding when to pump and how much. Some mothers pump on one side while the baby is nursing on the other. This is most effective because these moms have less difficulty relaxing themselves to experience the let-down reflex.

Just as with bottles, there is no one ideal make, model, or mechanism of pump that is ideal for all women. If there were, there would be only one model you could buy. If pumping isn't going well with a particular type of pump, consider getting a different brand. If electric isn't working for you, try mechanical (or vice versa).

Pumping at work

Breast-pumping at work can be a problem. In the early twenty-first century, many employers claim to be friendly to nursing mothers, but they simply cannot provide the resources or space to make pumping possible. In my practice I had a mother who was a convention planner. Her job required her to travel to various convention halls and prepare them for incoming vendors and displays. Finding privacy in convention halls proved to be a daunting task for this mom. The only privacy she could find was in the small, usually inadequate bathrooms tucked in the corners of these huge buildings. She gave up after a few weeks. I've had a few mothers who've tried pumping in their cars when the workplace didn't provide adequate amenities. This, too, almost never worked, but at least the mothers tried.

There are at least as many success stories of mothers willing to think outside of the box (or outside the pumping room, if you prefer) as there are stories of failure. A mom in my practice returned to work almost immediately because she was a housecleaner and her livelihood depended on her continuing to work. This mom exclusively breast-fed her daughter for six months by taking her daughter with her to all of her client's homes. The client was never there when she was so privacy was never an issue. And it's quite possible that the sound of the vacuum cleaner provided a nice white noise machine for the baby between feedings.

Many mothers nurse at home and have another caregiver feed formula to the baby while they are at work. The standard objection to this is that the baby will develop *nipple confusion,* loss of the ability to nurse at her mother's nipple because getting milk from a bottle is so much easier. Before I started practicing pediatrics I believed in nipple confusion. Now I still believe in it, but I know that it is extremely rare. Most babies will gratefully accept milk, especially mother's milk, from any delivery mechanism. Fear of nipple confusion should not deter a mother from nursing at home and having the baby bottled-fed while she is at work.

Lactation consultants can be very helpful to moms trying to figure out how to continue nursing after returning to work. A bunch of moms in my practice share tips and tricks with their nursing friends. Finally, the ultimate source is the Internet, the true marketplace of ideas (good, bad, and indifferent). All these sources provide ideas from which you can derive your own formula for making breast-feeding and work go together.

Solid, Jackson (Starting Solids)

One of the most common questions I get at the four-month well-baby visit is about starting solids, and one of the most common reasons I get this question is because parents have already started feeding their baby solids by the time I see them for the four-month visit. That's why I often talk about solids at the two-month visit.

The only reason for having this discussion at four months of age is that your baby probably is capable of doing two things she needs to do before she can handle semisolids. She needs to be able to hold her head up by herself for several minutes, and she also needs to be able to use her tongue to move a semisolid mass of stuff from the front to the back of her mouth and then to swallow it.

The cons

Like many things in life, however, just because a person *can* do something doesn't mean he *should* do it.

The only thing a baby needs until six months of age is 20-calorie-per-ounce breast milk or formula. It's all she needs to develop properly and to grow well, particularly to grow her brain, which needs the fats and proteins provided by breast milk and formula. As a percentage of its ultimate size, the baby's brain is growing more rapidly in the first six months of life than at any other time. Babies and toddlers have such relatively large heads because their brains do most of their growing in the first two years of life. Of those first two years the most important months for growth are the first six months. I don't like to recommend anything that will compromise the baby's brain growth, such as sacrificing space in the baby's stomach that could otherwise be full of milk.

Another reason parents start solids at four months of age is that their own parents tell them to: "That's when I started giving you solids, and *you* turned out all right." In fact, there may be a chorus of voices telling you to start solids at four months, but your mother isn't your baby's mother—you are! You can take her advice if it seems right to you, but don't feel you need to take it because she is your mother.

Another reason to hold off is a theoretical one. Some experts believe that the baby's immature intestine should not be exposed to anything more complex than milk for more or less the first six months. This is because in theory the barrier between inside and outside the baby's body is not as tight as it will be later in life. There is at least a theoretical risk of molecules crossing into the baby's bloodstream that could promote the development of allergies.

Finally, some people will tell you that when the baby starts showing interest in the food you're eating, it's time to feed her solids. This is a myth. Of course your baby is going to be interested in your food. Food is intrinsically interesting stuff. Just because your baby shows interest in your food doesn't mean she should eat it.

The pros

There are a couple of reasons for starting solids early that, while not ideal reasons, are at least rational.

The first has to do with a strange and wonderful fact about modern society: We are victims of our own success. For babies, that means that many of them are so healthy and, as a result, grow more quickly than we were ever meant to grow. Some babies actually outgrow the caloric endowment that 20-calorie-per-ounce breast milk or formula can provide. This used to happen after six months of age when a baby would be starting solids anyway, so it never posed a problem. But now between four and six months, we're starting to see babies that seem to nurse or feed constantly and are waking up in the middle of the night when they used to sleep through the night (and not because they've been teething).

If it appears that your baby is nursing pretty much constantly, you're probably right: She's nursing almost constantly. For some four-to-six-month-olds, this is may be a phase that will only last a few days. If it continues longer than this you have two choices. You can tough it out until the baby reaches six months or you can start solids.

Another reason why starting solids would be rational has to do with moms who return to work at three months (thank you Family and Medical Leave Act). The schedule of these mothers has changed so that they cannot sleep as little as they had while on leave and also remain awake, alert, and productive at work. I can often tell who these mothers are at the four-month checkup because they appear exhausted and dehydrated. Many of them admit the first month back at work is turning them into physical and mental basket cases.

How to add solids

If you're going to start solids, here's how. Keeping in mind that your baby really only requires milk for her nutrition during the first six months, the object of starting solids is only to give her some more calories so that she'll sleep longer, or at least so that she'll give you longer stretches in which you can do something other than feed her. That being the case, you don't need to feed her anything fancier than rice cereal. In fact, rice cereal is probably the only solid she should take until she's six months old.

Rice cereal is relatively easy for babies to digest and is also unlikely to provoke an allergic reaction. That's not to say that your baby won't show at least some kind of reaction to this radical change in her diet. Some babies who start rice cereal get gassy or colicky. Some babies get bound up and constipated, at least temporarily. And for virtually all of them, their poop really starts to stink. If you thought baby poop smelled bad, steel yourself and hold your nose for rice-cereal poop!

Rice cereal for babies is commercially available and is relatively inexpensive. That's good, because you're likely to waste a fair amount of it in the early stages of experimenting with feeding. There's no particular brand that is any better than any other and no reason to prefer organic over nonorganic. Remember, this isn't going to be a major part of your baby's diet; it's just a temporary measure to hold her over until she starts eating solids in earnest.

You'll want to feed your baby rice cereal mixed with breast-milk or formula, using a small baby spoon. She should be sitting in a high chair to do this, with a bib around her neck, and a large drop cloth under the high chair to catch the inevitable mess.

Start by making the rice cereal–milk combination runny, almost like soup. As your baby gets better at handling solids, she'll be able to handle thicker mixtures, so you can adjust accordingly. At first, plan on giving between an ounce and two ounces of the runny cereal and milk mixture once a day.

The first spoonful may not go well. Your baby may make a face and spit it out. Some babies make a face every time you put the first spoonful in their mouth. Our first baby made a face at the first spoonful of every feeding, even if it was a food he had been eating for weeks. Don't give up. This is all new for your baby. She has a lot to get used to. It's possible that some of the first spoonfuls of rice cereal will actually end up in the baby's stomach and not on the bib or on the floor.

Timing

When is the best time to give rice cereal? With the introduction of rice cereal, many parents hope they'll achieve the desired effect of having a baby who is happy and content and who sleeps through the night. Sometimes it works, but sometimes it doesn't. It may help to move the rice cereal feeding a little closer to the hour of sleep. You don't want to do this too soon or too close to bedtime in case your baby gets colicky and gassy and her whole nighttime pattern gets thrown off. If your baby is doing well with rice cereal and you're thickening it up so it's more of a paste than a soup, you may be able to move the feeding closer to bedtime. If the experiment in better sleep just doesn't seem to be working, the best approach may be to back off solids and to try again at six months, when your baby will be better able to handle more complex foods.

If, no matter what you do, rice cereal doesn't seem to agree with your baby, there are other cereals to try. Babies also tolerate oatmeal well. If your baby was getting constipated with rice cereal, oatmeal may be a good alternative. Many parents ask me why they have to stick to cereal: Why can't we give baby food, like vegetables and fruits? You can give these things, but that doesn't mean you should. My recommendation at this age is to keep it simple and to keep in mind that the main purpose of solids is to give the baby more calories so you and she can get more sleep.

Rash Alert

Baby rashes are common, and most of them are not allergic rashes. Even fewer rashes are caused by milk-protein allergies. As a pediatrician, I find that some careful questioning and examination may provide clues as to what's an allergic reaction and what's not.

Food allergy rashes on babies tend to appear as *eczema*. Eczema is patches of dry, scaly skin that is sometimes red, sometimes yellow, and sometimes weeps clear fluid. The most common locations for eczema in babies are behind the ears, in the folds of the elbows, and behind the knees. Although this kind of eczema rash is common in babies and may occur for no discernible reason, an eczema rash that is more severe or covers a more extensive area on the baby's body might signal a milk-protein allergy.

Often, a baby with this allergic reaction is fussy or difficult to console. Some of these babies actually vomit forcefully after feeding as opposed to the normal spitting up that is so common in babies. If any of these things happen to your baby, whether your baby is breast-fed or bottle-fed, contact your pediatrician and begin investigating the possibility of a food allergy.

For breast-feeding mothers, a milk-protein allergy is obviously more complicated. The first step I recommend in these cases is to have mom eliminate all dairy from her diet. This is easier said than done. Elimination means 100% elimination. The mother has to cut out not only milk, cheese, and yogurt but also all products that contain the proteins whey and casein. This requires some careful label-reading. If after more than two days (remembering our rule) the baby's rash is improving, then I recommend that the mother stay off milk strictly for as long as she breast-feeds. Most of these babies will be able to consume dairy products without difficulty by their first birthday.

If milk elimination doesn't work, mom may need to eliminate soy and substitute other protein sources for herself. The more foods are eliminated, the more difficulty the mother will have feeding herself, so I recommend she does this with the help of her pediatrician, a nutritionist, or both.

Some protein allergies manifest themselves only as blood passed in the baby's poop. If you suspect your baby is passing blood, bring a diaper with the offending matter to the doctor to verify that it is indeed blood that your baby is pooping. After asking some questions and performing an exam, I usually recommend a milk-protein elimination trial. This usually solves the problem, and virtually all these babies outgrow their allergy.

You may have noticed that I have not recommended allergy testing. There are a couple of reasons for this. One is that, given the age of the baby, many of these tests will not be accurate and may be prone to false-negative or false-positive results. I usually prefer to perform what I call the "test of life," that is, eliminating the suspected allergen and looking at the result. Regardless of the outcome of an allergy test, presuming we could perform them in little babies, the test of life is the only test that matters. If a baby breaks out in a rash every time she drinks a milk-based formula or every time her mother nurses her after putting cream in her coffee, I don't really care what the allergy test shows. The test of life shows that she probably shouldn't be exposed to milk protein.

Aw, POOP!

There's a lot of mythology and lore about what normal baby poop should look like and even what it should smell like. I care a great deal more about what goes into a baby than I do about the color and consistency of what comes out of a baby. For breast-fed baby poop, almost any color and consistency may be normal. It will vary widely depending on what mom is eating. The only colors that aren't normal are red like blood and black like stereo equipment. Either of these may be signs of bleeding that should be addressed with your pediatrician.

I care even less about the consistency of poop. Parents often ask, "What about constipation, doctor?" For me, constipation has a different definition than for most people. I don't care as much about consistency and frequency as I care about *pain*. The classic teaching says that a normal, exclusively breast-fed baby may pass a large poop painlessly as infrequently as once per week!

On the other hand, if a baby poops three times per day, but only with great effort, and she spends the majority of that day straining and pushing and turning red trying to produce those poops, I'd say there is a problem that might require some fixing. The problem isn't consistency and frequency; the problem is pain.

For formula-fed babies (and for most breast-fed babies as well), the most common poop appearance is the classic mustard-seed yellow poop. The color may vary across the yellow and green portion of the spectrum. As for consistency, anything from the consistency of pure water to thick paste may be normal. As for frequency, I don't bother counting poops. It's a useless exercise that taxes your energy and doesn't give you any important information about how to feed your baby. However, if your regularly pooping baby suddenly becomes "backed-up" and seems uncomfortable, adding an ounce or two of diluted prune juice (one part juice to one part water) may provide some temporary relief and may jump-start her normal pattern.

Troubleshooting

My baby gets easily distracted

Even though eating is the most important activity in a baby's day, some babies are easily distracted by noise, particularly from pets or older siblings. Some mothers find that the baby is easily distracted by the television or the radio if she plays it while feeding or nursing. The fix is fairly simple: Try to create a sensory-poor environment in which to feed the baby. For some families this will be difficult, depending on the level of chaos already in the household. I recommend being creative and trying to come up with places and times to feed your baby where there will be minimal sound and light to distract her.

I'm making too much milk!

This is a nice problem to have. First, you should examine why you're making so much. You want to make sure you're not pumping more than you absolutely need to. Recall that breast-feeding is a demand-driven process, so if you pump more you'll make more. The same goes for mothers who are experiencing engorgement shortly after their milk comes in. I recommend that they express only enough milk to relieve the terrible pressure and no more, lest they set up a vicious cycle of pumping and engorgement.

Many mothers freeze pumped breast milk. Breast milk that is pumped and put directly in the freezer is good for up to nine months. For all intents and purposes, this is longer than you will need to use it. Even if you observe the "first in, first out" rule and thaw the oldest milk first, most mothers who pump and freeze end up running out of freezer space and throwing out old milk.

Some mothers ask about donating their unused breast milk to milk banks. There are several of these nationwide. There is a fairly extensive screening process that is involved in becoming a milk donor, but it may be well worth the effort. Because of the many known health benefits of human breast milk, many special-care nurseries and neonatal intensive care units have started giving donated breast milk to premature infants.

Teething and nursing

Mothers tell me there is no sensation quite like being bitten for the first time by your precious little baby who you didn't know had a sprouted a tooth. Mothers also tell me that babies quickly learn not to bite their mothers. How they do this is a mystery to me, whether by learned behavior, instinct, or a combination of the two. Mothers themselves will reflexively pull the baby off the breast when they are bitten. Babies seem to get the message soon after and stop biting mom. And that's a good thing for everybody.

What do I do with thawed breast milk that my baby doesn't finish?

It's probably safest to throw it out. Remember that breast milk is raw milk, which means it is unpasteurized. Therefore, as it's pumped the clock on its shelf life starts ticking. You can suspend that clock by freezing the milk, but once you thaw it again, it should be used right away or discarded.

What about formula that my baby doesn't finish?

The manufacturer recommends that you throw it out right away. But if you think about it, that's what you'd expect a manufacturer who wanted to sell more formula to say. I recommend immediately putting it in the refrigerator and using it at the next feeding, a maximum of three or four hours later.

I want my baby to sleep through the night. Can I add rice cereal to the bottle?

I don't recommend adding rice cereal to bottles unless you are doing so as part of the treatment of gastroesophageal reflux (see Chapter 8). If your child is less than four months old, I don't recommend adding cereal for supplement purposes. This is too much too soon. If the baby is four months or older and you feel you must give rice cereal (see earlier in this chapter), feed it to her with a spoon.

Notes:

- Why do babies cry?
- Once you've figured out why your baby is crying, what are the most common and popular soothing techniques?
- What is meant by self-soothing, and what does it mean for your role in calming your baby?
- How can you soothe a colicky baby?

Chapter 5

How to Soothe Your Baby and Calm Crying

So your baby is crying and you can't figure out why. This chapter will give you some explanations and strategies to help you through these tough moments with your new baby.

The Three Reasons

The bad news is that there are fewer sounds that are more difficult to listen to than your own baby crying. There may be ancient biological reasons for this. In any case, once you hear that cry from your own baby, you'll understand what I mean!

The good news is that there are really only three basic reasons why your baby is crying: She's hungry; she's uncomfortable (for instance, with gas or a wet diaper); or she just needs to be held (and not just held, but held in a certain way; see below). In any case, babies never cry for *no* reason. Come to think of it, *no one* cries for no reason. Even actors cry because they are getting paid to play a scene. With your baby, however, regardless of whether she is hungry, is uncomfortable, or needs to be held, the reason is basically the same: She wants something from you. It may be the case that babies have such piercing, plaintive, and just plain miserable cries precisely because that type of cry is likely to get a parent running to the crib. That's the point: The baby knows instinctively that crying is the best way to get her needs met.

Hunger

If two to three hours have passed since her last feeding and it's about time for the baby to eat, the baby may be crying from hunger. Generally, though, if a baby is crying from hunger, it's because she has already spent several minutes giving you other cues that she's hungry, such as stirring and rooting while possibly making cooing noises. If your baby has gotten to the point of crying, you've probably delayed too long to start the feeding. At this point your baby may be so frantic from hunger that it might prove difficult to calm her down. The paradox is that the baby may be too wound up to accomplish the very task she needs to do in order to calm down: eat!

In cases like this, I recommend looking for a brief window of opportunity when the baby stops crying. It's important that while waiting you don't become so wound up that neither the baby nor you can calm down enough to get her to feed! This may require a supreme act of self-control, but with practice you can get it done. The window of opportunity, when the baby is relatively calmer, is the time to introduce the nipple (human or otherwise) to the baby's mouth. She may fuss and cry a bit, but eventually she'll realize that there's milk there and she'll calm down the rest of the way.

What if she just fed? If much less than the usual interval has passed since the baby last fed and she had a good long feed at that time, it may be a mistake to try to feed her. Some mothers come to the mistaken conclusion that their own milk is not enough for their baby, so they try to supplement with formula at this point. Another downside to early feedings is that some rare babies may feed even when they are not particularly hungry. This may lead to overfeeding. An overfed baby is frequently gassy and spitty. Usually when you try to feed babies who are not really hungry, the problem is that they just wanted skin-to-skin attention; they will nurse for a few seconds and then calmly fall asleep. These are babies who weren't hungry after all.

Discomfort

Sometimes the baby will cry because she is feeling something uncomfortable. Many parents interpret these cries as being cries of pain. They probably are not. Cries of pain are more like the cries of shock and displeasure when the baby gets an injection. When I give shots in my office, many parents tell me that their baby has "never cried like that." I have no reason to doubt them. The child hasn't had routine vaccines before!

Babies who cry because of discomfort do so for several reasons. They could really hate the feeling of having a full diaper. Or maybe they hate being naked (or conversely, they hate being overly covered in clothes). Some babies cry because they don't like the sensation of being bathed. Most of these cries are pretty easy to figure out, since the pattern gets established fairly early in life. I recommend going down a mini-checklist to discover why the baby is uncomfortable. Many parents check the diaper first. Then they look for clues to see if the baby has a gas bubble or is struggling to make a poop. These babies will have stomachs that feel fuller than normal or will turn red, strain, and appear to bear down.

I learned a technique from parents in my practice who figured out on their own how to calm a baby who is struggling with intestinal distress. They start by taking one little leg in each hand and making little "bicycling" movements, and, if necessary, follow bicycling with a gentle belly massage. Even if these movements don't directly solve the problem (they probably don't), the baby finds the attention and the massage pleasurable, which is often enough to stop the crying.

Wardrobe Blues

For babies who cry because they hate being naked or hate having their clothes changed, I use a technique I learned from an obstetrician colleague: I place a thumb in the palm of each of the baby's hands and gently bring the little hands up to baby's mouth. Sometimes I try to gently insert one of the baby's knuckles in her mouth so that she can begin to suck. Failing that, I try to introduce the tip of my pinky finger upside down into the roof of the baby's mouth so that she'll suck. Usually if she starts to suck she'll calm down quickly.

The Brazilian cure: There are a host of culturally specific techniques for calming a crying baby who isn't hungry but just needs to poop or pass a gas bubble. In Brazil, the crying therapy of choice is to feed the baby a little dilute tea.

The tea of choice in Brazil is *erva doce* ("sweet herb"). Americans know sweet herb as anise, the principal ingredient in licorice. Having tasted *erva doce*, I can attest that it tastes nothing at all like licorice. Some Brazilians prefer chamomile, but *erva doce* remains the national favorite. Brazilian moms make a dilute batch of tea and serve it one ounce at a time in a bottle at room temperature.

After ten years of seeing Brazilian families in my practice, I now recommend *erva doce* to parents who ask me what they can give to a baby with bound up intestines or gas. Many of these parents are relieved to hear the recommendation because they have already tried it, but I always add a couple pieces of "American" advice regarding the Brazilian cure.

First, since I want to make sure the baby is getting enough breast milk or formula, I counsel parents to limit the tea dose to one ounce no more than three times per day.

Second, I employ a trick I learned in the special-care nursery from the nurses taking care of preemies. In the special-care nurseries, the nurses noted that sugar-water served as a calming agent, even as a pain-reducer, prior to painful procedures such as needle sticks. It turns out that in babies younger than two months, sugar appears to act as a laxative, a calming agent, and an all-purpose, fussy-baby remedy. I recommend adding one level teaspoon of sugar to the ounce of tea. If that sounds sweet, it is. The mixture is the equivalent of 5% glucose solutions that hospital nurses use prior to painful procedures.

What NOW?

Tea, Honey, or Sugar?

If it turns out that sugar is the "active ingredient" in this all-purpose intestinal cure, you could reasonably ask whether you can simply give your baby sugar-water and save the trouble of making tea. The answer is that you can, but don't make such a suggestion to a Brazilian mom. In Brazil many believe that giving sugar to babies causes intestinal worms.

Brazilians would much rather give honey than sugar, but virtually all of them have heard that we don't give honey to babies in the U.S. Most, however, don't know the reason why honey is off-limits for babies. It turns out that honey, especially honey made in small batches at local farms, is susceptible to contamination with spores from *Clostridium botulinum*, the causative agent of the paralytic infection botulism. Babies older than one year tend to be large enough to withstand the effects of the usually small number of botulinum spores associated with commercially available honey.

I just want to be held. Is that so wrong?

Once hunger and discomfort have been eliminated from the checklist, there remains the baby who cries because she wants to be held (actually there is one other reason babies cry—classic colic, which I'll explore in more detail below).

The baby who wants to be held seldom wants to be simply held. Usually she will only accept being held when you are standing up. You figure this out quickly when you try to sit down. But it can be tougher than this. Not only does the baby want you to hold her while you're standing up, but you need to walk—and this usually happens between the hours of 2:00 a.m. and 4:00 a.m. No one really knows why some babies go through periods when they want to be held, but everyone has his or her own ideas. My personal theory is that babies have an innate need for human contact. For most of human history babies enjoyed almost uninterrupted contact with their mothers. If that contact was broken briefly the baby was usually okay. After all, mom needed to go to the bathroom, eat, and bathe. But eventually the baby needed the care, comfort, and protection of a pair of arms, so she cried to get it back. The fact that a baby needs to be held while a parent is standing up and walking might be a legacy of our mobile ancestors, who were often on the move and carried their infants strapped tightly to their bodies.

Special Cases

Some cries are different from the cries described above. In these cases, the baby really does appear to be in pain, as though she is getting shots, without apparent reason. In such cases, there are some particular signs worth looking for. I recommend removing all the baby's clothes and examining her carefully. Pay particular attention to the fingers and toes. What you're looking for are "hair tourniquets."

A hair tourniquet occurs when a piece of hair, either from the baby or someone else, becomes wrapped tightly around the base of a baby's finger or toe. The indentation will be clearly visible. The circulation to the affected digit can be affected, causing painful swelling. This is why the baby is crying. Hair tourniquets are fairly easy to remove manually or with the help of a tweezers. If you can't get the hair off yourself, you may need to consult a physician about how to proceed. Once you've removed the hair, you may notice that it cut the skin on the baby's digit. I recommend placing an antibiotic ointment on the cut toe or finger three times per day for a few days until it is healed.

Other kinds of crying may indicate more serious conditions. If the baby cries inconsolably and then relaxes only to begin crying inconsolably several minutes later, the problem may be intestinal. If the baby then passes stool that looks bloody or like currant jelly, the reason for the crying may be one of several kinds of intestinal obstruction that require emergent medical attention.

What Is "Inconsolable" Crying?

To a pediatrician, inconsolable crying means crying for 30 minutes without stopping even for the briefest moment. By this definition, most baby crying is not inconsolable. This is because crying from most of the common causes usually involves pauses of a few seconds every few minutes.

What Is "Projectile Vomiting"?

Unfortunately, as one of my colleagues once remarked, in most people's minds "projectile vomiting" is any vomit that comes out of their child's mouth. That's why pediatricians are trained to ask parents what they mean by "projectile." Several inches doesn't count. If the stuff flies off the end of the bed, or at least five or six feet, that is projectile. This merits a call to the doctor.

Crying associated with certain kinds of vomiting also may merit medical attention. If the baby spits up yellow or green, this may also indicate a type of intestinal obstruction that merits attention. If, when the baby throws up, she is able to hurl milk five or six feet, we define this as "projectile vomiting." This too deserves urgent attention.

If the crying is associated with fever, poor feeding, or any kind of abnormal appearance or abnormal behavior during the non-colicky times of the day (2:00 a.m. to 10:00 p.m.) when the baby should be acting normally, these are warning signs that you should probably contact your pediatrician.

Finally, colic and reflux often overlap. If a baby is fussy and cries all day long, not only at night, and is especially fussy during and after feedings, reflux could be to blame. If the baby has a tendency to arch, make grimacing faces, and even turn colors after eating, even if she doesn't spit up, the problem could be reflux. I cover reflux in more detail in Chapter 8.

An Overview of Soothing Techniques

All soothing techniques begin with good detective work on the part of the parents. Why is the baby crying? Once hunger and discomfort have been investigated and ruled out, there are a number of other questions to be addressed. First, a few words about things babies need. Until about four to six months of age, a baby lacks the means to soothe herself into a calm state. That is to say, she requires something *outside her own body* to help her regulate her state to quiet for feeding or sleep. Some babies require more outside assistance than others, but all babies require at least a small amount. On average, girls acquire self-soothing earlier than boys. Girls tend to accomplish the task after about four months; boys, after about six months.

Does your baby need to be swaddled?

Swaddling, or wrapping a baby firmly in a blanket, is one of the most ancient soothing techniques. Swaddling requires a piece of fabric (or in the old days, animal skin). Wrapping an infant but not carrying her is relatively new in human history. The most prevalent theory explaining why swaddling soothes a crying baby is that a firmly wrapped baby feels as though she is still in the womb, where she felt warm, safe, and comfortable for several months before birth. Of course, the differences between a swaddling blanket and the womb are stark: The latter is wet, hot, and pitch black, and the baby isn't breathing air.

I recommend wrapping up the baby's legs with all the joints in the flexed position: hips, knees, and ankles. Wrapped like this, the baby does indeed appear as she did when she was still in mom's uterus, at least for the last several weeks as she was growing larger.

Swaddling your baby

Place baby on a large, lightweight blanket with the top corner folded down.

Fold one corner over the baby.

Tuck the end under the baby.

Bring the bottom corner up and over the baby's shoulder.

Fold the other side corner over the baby.

Tuck the end under the baby.

What about the arms? This is a question that parents frequently ask me, virtually always because their baby has a tendency to struggle to free her hands from the swaddling blanket. Some theories suggest that you should tightly wrap the arms just like the legs. I don't subscribe to this school of thought. In my experience, some babies simply will not calm down unless their arms are free. My advice to these parents is that if the baby fights her arms out of the swaddling *and then she becomes calm*, it makes no sense to reswaddle her arms.

The binky

One of the best ways to soothe a fussy baby is to allow her to suck on something. Sucking is likely *the most* ancient soothing method known to humankind. Throughout human history, the sucking device of choice has been the human nipple, and, in fact, the proximity of mother and baby made the nipple an easily accessible and available choice.

In modern times, necessity gave birth to a number of inventions to replace mother's breast, at least for short stretches of time. The human finger, as described above, was a good temporary device provided it was properly clean. Some lucky babies learn to suck a knuckle or a finger, but the majority are not coordinated enough in the first four to six months to do this consistently. This is why I am a big fan of the pacifier *until six months of age*. After that time, I recommend removing the binky from the house and throwing it as far away as you can.

The first artificial pacifier appeared in seventeenth-century England in the form of a corncob that could be cut down to a size appropriate for a baby's mouth. These early pacifiers were followed by rattles fitted with bits of animal bone about the size of a nipple. The rubber nipple pacifier arrived with the Industrial Revolution in the mid-nineteenth century.

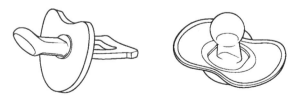

There are any number of pacifier models on the market. Experiment and see which works best for your baby. Using a silicone pacifier avoids any potential allergic reactions to latex ones.

Controversy regarding pacifier use dates to the advent of the pediatrician in the early twentieth century. Binkies were felt to be unsanitary (to be sure, this was often true), and many believed that their use damaged the baby's normal psychological development, (which was subsequently shown to be untrue).

The objections to pacifier use with more solid scientific backing were the findings that showed disturbance in tooth development in babies who used the binky beyond one year of life. Finally, there is the suggestion that pacifier use interferes with the process of nursing. My professional experience with nursing babies and pacifiers has been that this is untrue. I find that virtually no babies who use pacifiers have difficulty nursing. To the contrary: Some babies so badly need to suck when they are not nursing that if they do not use an artificial device, they will need to use their mother as their pacifier. I have yet to meet a mother who enjoys being her baby's pacifier!

My own recommendations regarding using the pacifier to soothe a fussy baby are as follows: As long as the baby is in that phase of her life during which she requires something external to her body to help her stay calm, the binky can be a very good thing indeed. Once the baby begins to develop her own internal means of self-soothing (around four months for girls, closer to six months for boys), however, the pacifier loses its usefulness and should be tossed out.

The last thing parents want is for a child who could have quickly and easily separated from her pacifier to become addicted to it by nine months of age. Parents also want to avoid the baby needing the binky as a sleep association (see Chapter 6). I recommend using six months as a hard deadline for getting rid of the pacifier. The transition to self-soothing will be much smoother if you do.

Rock. On.

Many parents ask about rocker devices, particularly parents who have already purchased rockers. Rockers are perfectly fine from the earliest infancy provided the baby likes them. If the baby hates being in the rocker, no parent would keep her in there for long. A variation on the rocker is the vibrating bouncy seat. Many parents enjoy great success using the vibrating seat as a soothing device. And of course there is the original rocker, the rocking chair, though a rocking chair requires an adult to sit in it first. A terrific modern variation on the classic rocker is the glider, which gives a smooth and safe ride for baby and parent. Like any location where you place a baby—with the exception of bassinets and cribs—these soothing devices require constant parental supervision.

Bye-bye car-car

Some parents discover the only way they can get their baby to sleep is to give her a ride in the car. The car can be an effective technique. The major problems with the car should be fairly obvious: Most likely a sleep-deprived, stressed parent with an at least initially crying baby in the back seat will be driving the car at night. This is a dangerous thing to do. The parent doing the driving should first assure himself or herself that he or she is calm, cool, and collected; that the car is in good working order with working heat or AC; and that the roads he or she will be driving are safe.

The "C" Word

Colic deserves special mention here. No one knows what colic is or what causes it, but it is defined by the "colic rule of three": Colic begins at about three weeks of age and lasts until about three months. The baby cries for at least three hours at a time, usually at the worst possible hours of the day, from 10:00 p.m. to about 2:00 a.m. The crying occurs at least three days out of the week for at least three weeks. The key feature of colic is that the colicky baby is perfectly normal and feeds normally during the non-colicky hours of the day.

What causes colic?

The word *colic* derives from the word from which we derive the anatomic term *colon*, suggesting that classically colic was believed to derive from intestinal distress. But there are many reasons to believe that gas, constipation, and intestinal floral composition has nothing to do with colic. Babies appear to be just as gassy or as constipated before a colicky period as they are after it.

Premature infants do not become colicky until they reach the age that makes them three weeks older than their due date. Babies born ill and those born healthy seem to have similar rates of colic. And the psychological state of the parent seems to correlate poorly with colic. Colic, however, has a way of adding substantial stress to an already stressful environment and can provoke depression in mothers as well as marital stress.

Old-School Colic Therapies

The practice of drugging crying babies dates back to the earliest Greek physicians. Galen reportedly recommended opium to stop babies from crying. The treatment withstood the test of time because, by the Middle Ages, mothers and wet nurses were still using opium, now as pastes and ointments smeared on their breasts. Ethanol, in the form of whiskey and bourbon, was also commonly used well into the twentieth century.

The dawn of the pharmaceutical age in the twentieth century saw powerful sedatives being given to even the smallest babies to "cure" colic. Doctors frequently prescribed phenobarbital, valium, and antispasmodic drugs such as scopolamine. Use of all these drugs was discontinued when it was discovered that they were dangerous and even deadly for infants.

In the early twentieth century, Luther Emmett Holt, then the dean of American Pediatrics, championed the "cry-it-out" approach. Dr. Benjamin Spock gave the technique further credibility in the earliest editions of *Baby and Child Care,* though later editions abandoned the approach. Today, no expert, including Ferber, advocates allowing a baby to cry to the point of exhaustion.

Harvey Karp: *The Happiest Baby on the Block*

Dr. Harvey Karp provides a compelling explanation for why colic occurs. Dr. Karp believes that babies are born three months early, mostly because human heads grow so rapidly in utero. He argues that the baby must be born three months early or risk becoming stuck in the birth canal.

According to Dr. Karp, because the baby is "born three months early" she isn't fully prepared to be here in the bright, noisy, rough-and-tumble world. As a result, the baby has fussy periods during those times of the day (actually at night) when she would have otherwise been soothed in the tight, warm environment of the uterus.

It's a compelling theory, though it has a few holes. Karp doesn't have a satisfying explanation for why colic doesn't begin at birth instead of at three weeks. Karp's theory also ignores the timing of human lung development, which is such that lungs are fully mature and capable of breathing room air between 34 and 35 weeks gestation. If babies are meant to be born at 52 weeks instead of 40, it doesn't make sense that lungs would be ready to breathe room air four months earlier than they need to be. Nature doesn't waste time and energy on unnecessary development.

Finally, though Karp's soothing techniques (more on these below) work great for colicky babies, they also work great for babies less than three weeks old, before the classic colic period begins. Newborns on the first day of life calm easily when swaddled, placed on their side, and so on.

As for babies older than four months, Karp is right that they no longer require these special soothing techniques because these babies have begun to acquire their own internal soothing mechanisms. A typical four-month-old girl, for example, can be laid down in her crib awake and allowed to fuss herself rapidly to sleep. It's also the case that four-month-olds as a rule do not require swaddling, though many will require sucking if the habit is not discouraged.

One final criticism of Karp's theory derives from his suggestion that there are several communities in the world where colic is unknown. All the communities named in *Happiest Baby*, by any measure, are medically and technologically impoverished societies in which women remain either pregnant or lactating from the time of menstruation until their deaths, the latter often occurring during childbirth. We may stipulate that colic doesn't occur in these cultures, probably because babies are carried next to their mothers 24 hours a day for the first several months of life. Babies are constantly swaddled, sucking, and comforted by the movement of mom's body and the sound of her heartbeat. But the absence of colic comes at a cultural price that I suspect most modern women are unwilling to pay. It disturbs me that my colleague Dr. Karp presents these societies as exemplars of anti-colic parenting.

Having said all that, the Karp technique works!

Assuming that you've ruled out hunger and discomfort as the reason for your baby's crying, and that it's pretty clear your baby is suffering from classic colic according to the "rule of threes," then Dr. Karp's soothing techniques come in handy and are relatively easy to learn. The basis of Karp's soothing techniques is that they trigger a "calming reflex" that tricks the baby into feeling as if she is safe and warm in the womb. Karp's system is based on five maneuvers he calls the "five S's."

- *Swaddling*: Tight swaddling recreates the confinement of the womb.
- *Side/Stomach position*: Holding the baby on the right side slightly face down aids in calming her.

- *Shushing*: Karp uses a loud "ssh" sound similar to the sound of mother's circulation heard in the womb.
- *Swinging (and jiggling)*: Gentle but constant jiggling (especially of the head) is intended to remind babies of the constant motion they experienced in the womb.
- *Sucking*: Karp agrees with me regarding the use of pacifiers.

The good news

Colic ends. If you can make it through those difficult three months, you can probably endure anything that parenthood throws at you. Most parents find methods to manage colic that are inventions of their own or that build upon methods outlined in this and other baby books. Many parents pick up helpful tips from friends who've been through colic themselves.

Because every child is different, every child with colic is different. Soothing a colicky baby is a process that is usually best accomplished by the people who know their baby better than anybody else on Earth: her parents.

Chapter Highlights

- How can you tell if your baby is getting enough sleep?
- How can you get your baby to sleep?
- When can you start trying to schedule naps and nighttime sleep?
- What are sleep associations, and how do they affect your baby's sleep?
- How do you encourage good sleep associations and wean your baby from bad ones?

Chapter 6

Getting Baby to Sleep

Oh sleep! It is a gentle thing,
Beloved from pole to pole!
To Mary Queen the praise be given!
She sent the gentle sleep from Heaven,
That slid into my soul

(Samuel Taylor Coleridge, *The Rime of the Ancient Mariner*)

During the course of a well-child visit in my office, there are three topics I'm always sure to bring up (if a parent doesn't mention them first). They are diet, exercise, and sleep. These are the three legs on which all of pediatrics stands. If a child is eating a nutritious diet, getting a good amount of exercise, and sleeping well, the child tends to be healthy. If parents are having problems with any of the three "legs," I try to fix them, knowing that all three are essential to having a healthy, happy child.

Because newborns don't exercise much, for the zero-to-six-month group the discussions are all about diet and sleep. We discussed healthy eating in Chapter 4. Here we will discuss sleep, that most misunderstood and underappreciated of human functions.

Nuts and Bolts: Sleep Happens

Sleep is one of the three things you can't make a child do (the other two are eat and poop on the potty, but these are subjects for different books). Sleep is defined simply as the absence of consciousness and cessation of most voluntary muscle activity. Yet sleep is more complex than this definition, since it is generally accepted that all our senses are working while we sleep, and people who sleepwalk almost certainly are using their voluntary muscles!

New parents: Listen up! One thing we know for sure about sleep is that it is essential. Humans need sleep. Bad things happen to us when we don't sleep. The same thing goes for most of the animal kingdom. All animals sleep, even fish. If sleep were not essential, we might find animals that don't need to sleep after long periods of staying awake, but there are no such animals.

Knowing that sleep is essential, however, is not the same as knowing what sleep is *for*. The truth is that no one really knows why we need to sleep. Yet we spend about a third of our lives asleep. What is going on while we sleep?

Compelling scientific data suggest that, in general, sleep is restorative to the body's functions. That is to say, sleep helps the body "put itself back together" after a day of activity. It repairs and rebuilds. This goes for our immune systems as well, which may explain why people report becoming ill more often when they are sleep-deprived.

Babies are a special class of sleeping humans. They sleep far more than we do. Babies less than a month old may sleep 18 to 20 hours a day. The rest of the time they spend eating. During their first six months, babies sleep 14 to 18 hours a day and spend increasingly more of the day when they are not eating interacting with us and their environments. We don't know why babies sleep so much, but it could be that sleep is important for their developing brains.

Many parents ask me how they can tell if their baby is getting enough sleep. The question is difficult to answer without asking some more questions. How well is the baby eating? (This is often the first question I ask in response to most queries from parents on any subject.) Generally, a baby who eats well also sleeps well, and vice versa. Is the baby waking up on her own, or are you waking her up? Except when trying to get the process of breast-feeding going (see Chapter 4), it's almost never a good idea to wake a sleeping baby! Finally, how much sensory stimulation is there in the baby's world? Too much sound, light, and handling can overstimulate a baby and interrupt quality sleep. Parents may ask another version of the same question: whether their baby is getting too much sleep. Fortunately. this is never the case. It is impossible for a baby to get too much sleep unless she stays asleep and never wakes up, a situation obviously beyond the scope of this book.

So, What's Normal?

Since infants don't sleep in the same way that older children and adults do, it's difficult at times to tell the difference between normal and abnormal sleep. I get a lot of questions from parents about sleep patterns that are quite normal... for babies. Even though a newborn may sleep 20 hours out of 24, she sleeps for relatively short intervals (two to three hours) and then wakes up to eat. Since many of those waking intervals occur in the middle of the night when you would be expecting to sleep, you may get the impression that something is amiss.

Another endearing habit that babies have is a tendency to swap day and night. They are alert and playful for what seems like a lot of time at 2:00 a.m., but at 2:00 p.m. will eat quickly and immediately fall asleep. Everyone knows that babies reverse day and night, but no one knows why. A sleep specialist I asked about this habit told me that the truth lies somewhere between reality and perception. Although it's true that babies do tend to have more alert periods in the middle of the night, we are so unaccustomed to being awake at that hour that we get a false impression that the baby has reversed a normal sleep-wake cycle. The truth is simply that the baby only sleeps for two to three hours at a time and then wakes up.

How do you know if this already-difficult sleeping arrangement is normal or if the baby isn't sleeping enough? Rely on the eat-well, sleep-well formula. If your newborn baby nurses or takes the bottle hungrily for 10 to 15 minutes, she's probably eaten enough and should go back to sleep fairly quickly. If instead your baby stays up and cries and can't be consoled, that's a problem that we'll deal with later in this chapter and in Chapter 8 (on illness). For me, the baby's eating status trumps her sleep schedule. A baby who eats well and appears happy but who is apparently not sleeping enough is not a baby I worry about as much as one who is not eating well.

Getting Your Baby to Fall Asleep: A Broken Legacy

Contrary to popular belief, the current methods of helping tired parents get their babies to go to sleep are not current at all. The basic mechanisms of getting babies to sleep have changed little since the dawn of time. Experienced parents figured out methods that work ages ago and have been passing down the secrets one to another for centuries. The problem is that the chain of information has been broken. We wait longer to have children than we did in the past, and by the time we have children we no longer live with (or even near) the experienced parents who helped us through this period in the past. In the place of experienced parents to tell us what to do, we have books and the Internet.

The Strategies: A Brief Rundown of the Most Popular Go-to-Sleep Methods

Just as there are many common misconceptions about getting babies to sleep, there are many misconceptions about the many books written on the subject and the methods they propose. The reality is that there are more similarities among sleep methods than there are differences. In my practice, I have parents who are devotees of practically every sleep method published in the last 50 years, and each method occasionally goes wrong. When these methods go wrong, they tend to go wrong for the same reasons. I'll detail the most popular methods and give my synthesis of these sleep solutions below.

In my opinion, there are really only two major baby sleep methods: parent-directed and baby-directed. Parent-directed sleep methods are the older of the two, first published by pediatrician Emmet Holt in *The Care and Feeding of Children* in 1895. Prior to the middle of the last century, parent-directed sleeping techniques were the only ones pediatricians officially endorsed. It is unclear how parents actually dealt with their babies, however, since *they* were not publishing, and there was no Internet.

Holt's book gave parents the standard professional advice for the times, which was to place babies on a strict sleep schedule whether the baby was sleepy or not and to feed the baby on a strict schedule (including prescribed amounts and varieties) whether the baby was hungry or not. At the time, these were considered "scientific" recommendations and were based on the most current "research" of the late nineteenth and early twentieth centuries. It turns out, however, that there was nothing at all scientific about these recommendations, even if they did emanate from Harvard Medical School. They were nothing more than the expert opinions of physicians claiming to be authorities on the care and feeding of children.

Fortunately, the era of feeding and bedding down the baby on a clockwork schedule is over. Since the middle of the twentieth century, no reputable expert recommends ignoring your baby's cries. This includes those methods that have been labeled (incorrectly, in my view) "cry-it-out" methods. Contrary to popular belief, no expert recommends allowing your baby to cry to the point of exhaustion. In truth, there is no such thing as a cry-it-out method. The differences between baby-directed sleep methods and parent-directed sleep methods are subtle and almost stylistic. In general, every reputable expert recommends paying attention to your baby's cues, be they sleep cues or hunger cues.

The Parent-Directed Method

Briefly, parent-directed sleep methods are those in which caregivers provide substantial input regarding the baby's sleep patterns.

Gary Ezzo and Robert Bucknam: *On Becoming Babywise: Giving your infant the gift of nighttime sleep*

The most salient criticisms that have been leveled against this book have focused not on the method it describes but rather on the religious faith of Gary Ezzo. Mr. Ezzo is an unapologetic evangelical Christian, but one can read *Babywise* cover to cover and locate no hint of a religious worldview. If public buzz about parent-directed sleep methods has turned against *Babywise*, it has done so for the wrong reasons. In fact, the method is eminently reasonable and practical (and, I stress, nonreligious).

The *Babywise* method is based on the commonsense observation that a baby who has just finished a good feeding is probably not hungry. If, one hour later, the baby starts fussing and crying, many experienced parents understand that what is bothering the baby cannot be hunger because the baby just ate. As opposed to the attachment methods (see William Sears, below), *Babywise* suggests that parents first seek to find out what's bothering the baby before reflexively feeding her.

This is what happens in the real world. What mother has not looked into the bassinet at her crying baby who nursed an hour earlier and thought, "You can't be hungry, I just fed you," and then proceeded to see if the baby had gas or needed to be changed?

Babywise and other parent-directed methods also recognize a fact of life about babies: They are not born knowing how to get along in this world, including how they should eat and sleep. Babies need to be nudged, gently, in the direction of sleeping when it's time to sleep and eating when it's time to eat. This may involve staying with the baby for a few minutes to stroke her back, sing to her, or give her a fingertip to suck on. I believe that even parents dedicated to attachment methods recognize this truth and do a fair bit of nudging of the baby themselves, though they might not acknowledge it. It is, after all, our responsibility to teach our children how to be in this world.

The Baby-Directed Sleep Revolution

Baby-directed methods let the baby "call the shots" about when sleeping will occur, without input from caregivers.

Benjamin Spock: *Baby and Child Care*

The baby-directed sleep revolution began in 1946 when Benjamin Spock published *The Common Sense Book of Baby and Child Care*. Later editions were known simply as *Baby and Child Care*, and generations of readers know the book simply as *Spock*.

Dr. Spock's major contribution to the world of sleep training was the commonsense observation that exclusively parent-driven attempts to place a baby on a schedule don't appear to work. These babies tend to neither sleep well nor eat well. Spock's advice sounds reasonable—even obvious—to a modern reader, so it is difficult to imagine just how radical his ideas appeared to the mid-twentieth-century reader. But Spock's approach caught on. By 1998, *Baby and Child Care* had sold more than 50 million copies and had been translated into at least 38 languages. Spock spawned several generations of baby books (including this one) that trace their origins back to his teachings.

Although Spock did a great service to modern parents by freeing them from the strictures of "scientific" pediatrics, a few of his opinions about sleep brought him some justified criticism.

Spock argued that a baby should always sleep on her stomach (and later on her side) because if a baby were to spit up, she might choke on her spit-up. This was never true except in rare instances. Healthy, especially full-term, babies are fully capable of protecting their airways when they spit up. Ironically, it was scientific medicine that tripped up Spock. Large epidemiological studies of Sudden Infant Death Syndrome (SIDS) demonstrated a strong correlation between stomach sleeping and SIDS. Since "Back to Sleep" campaigns began in 1994, there has been a dramatic drop in SIDS deaths. The nature of the intervention was simply a recommendation to place babies flat on their backs, without pillows or cushions, to go to sleep. Later versions of *Baby and Child Care* were modified to acknowledge the evidence-based "back to sleep" recommendation.

Another peculiarity of Spock's was his insistence that children sleep through the night in their own bedrooms, even if there are only two children. It's quite possible that Spock's recommendation was a reaction to his own mother's insistence that he and his five siblings sleep together on a "sleeping porch," exposed to fresh air (actually cold air most of the year, since Spock grew up in New Haven, Connecticut). Though he rejected the notion of children sleeping together (and of children sleeping with their parents), Spock never lost his affection for fresh air, a recommendation that survived beyond the 50th anniversary of his book.

Richard Ferber: *Solve Your Child's Sleep Problems*

Perhaps the most famous, and easily the most misunderstood, of the modern sleep books is *Solve Your Child's Sleep Problems* (1986) by Richard Ferber of Children's Hospital, Boston. The "Ferber Method," as it is sometimes called, is historically associated (incorrectly, in my view) with the cry-it-out (in other words, parent-directed) method attributed to Emmet Holt.

Before discussing Ferber, it is important to specify which period of a child's developmental life we are discussing. Like all pediatrics, the age of the child guides the recommendation. Until somewhere between four and six months of age, a baby has no internal means of soothing herself. Girls acquire self-soothing earlier than boys on average. Girls tend to accomplish the task at about four months; boys accomplish it at about six months. Prior to this age, babies require help from something outside themselves. Some lucky babies learn to suck a knuckle or a finger, but the majority are not coordinated enough at this stage to do this consistently. This is why I am a big fan of the pacifier *until six months of age*. After that time, I recommend removing the "binky" from the house.

Many parents I have spoken to claim to have tried to "Ferberize" their babies (how many pediatricians do you know whose names have been turned into verbs?). Many of them identify Ferber with the cry-it-out method. By and large, these are parents who have not actually read *Solve Your Child's Sleep Problems* and have missed Ferber's most important message.

Richard Ferber is famous (or infamous, in the opinion of some) for the wrong reasons. In my experience, Ferber is famous for two tables detailing the number of minutes one should wait before reentering the room of a sleeping child. In my opinion, Ferber's "Story of the Pillow" far outweighs the tables in importance.

The pillow story is all about *sleep associations*—those sensations that a baby associates with falling asleep. All of us associate falling asleep with certain tactile sensations, amounts of light, and levels of sound. Starting between four and six months of age, when a baby begins to develop her own internal methods of self-soothing, she also starts developing sleep associations based on the things that surround her when she falls asleep.

All our sleep is characterized by rises and falls through deep and shallow sleep. When we get to the shallow levels of sleep, as we do every two to three hours, we are actually partially awake. In this state, we take a mental inventory of our sleep associations. If we find them all present, we roll over, fall deeper asleep, and never remember we were partially awake.

In the pillow story, Dr. Ferber asks the reader to imagine that during sleep your partner steals your pillow from you. When you get to that shallow level of sleep, you take a mental inventory: "Okay, it's dark, I'm in bed, I've got my pillow, now I'm going to roll over and... No! Wait a minute, where's my pillow?" And by now you're wide awake. You get ticked off, rummage around for your pillow, grab it back from your partner, and fall back to sleep. Ferber now has us imagine that once you're fast asleep your partner does the deed a second time! Once again, you get to shallow sleep, fail to find your pillow, and the cycle repeats.

This is precisely what happens with babies who require pacifiers or who need to nurse in order to fall asleep. Like us, they need to be surrounded by those things that will be there in three hours when they cycle once again into shallow sleep. If the pacifier falls out of the baby's mouth or if she gets to partial consciousness and notices she is no longer nursing (because mom is trying to get some sleep herself), she will awaken again, and this time she'll likely start crying.

The essence of the Ferber method is the elimination of adverse sleep associations. The crying that has become linked to the Ferber method is the understandable discomfort that the baby feels during the process of shedding an adverse sleep association. I view the table that has made Ferber (in)famous as a guide to helping your baby get over the process of losing sleep associations that don't allow her to learn to use her own internal soothing techniques.

Keep in mind that "Ferberization" does not work on the baby who has not yet developed her own internal self-soothing techniques. For this reason, it is futile to try to Ferberize a baby prior to four months of age.

If there is a downside to the Ferber Method, it is that the parents must endure some crying. I've recommended Ferber's book to several parents. Those who read the book find the method easy to understand and many are surprised to discover that the method works!

It is important to understand why the crying is necessary. If the baby had not acquired an adverse sleep association in the first place, the method would be unnecessary. In my view, the classic Ferber method does not apply to children with good sleep associations. For children with other sleep issues, it is necessary to explore, usually with your pediatrician, what might be keeping your baby up.

Marc Weissbluth: *Healthy Sleep Habits, Happy Child: A step-by-step program for a good night's sleep*

Dr. Weissbluth's book is an excellent complement to Dr. Ferber's. Both authors walk the tired parent through the mechanics of a baby's sleep, describing the various stages and their meanings. In *Healthy Sleep Habits, Happy Child: A step-by-step program for a good night's sleep*, Dr. Weissbluth's major contribution to the literature is his emphasis on the dangers of overstimulation and fatigue that follow from unhealthy sleep habits.

Dr. Weissbluth's other major contribution is his detailed descriptions of a baby's sleep and hunger cues and how to read them. The Dr. Weissbluth baby-directed sleep method posits that babies need to learn to sleep, but that this learning process is natural and parents should not interfere with it. My own opinion is that there is a fine line between "nudging" and interference on the part of parents. That line can and should be approached but not crossed. Parents should, in my opinion, help their babies develop healthy sleep habits, but, of course, parents cannot force this learning process.

Dr. Weissbluth does not advocate a cry-it-out method: "No parent wants her child to cry. The truth is that encouraging healthy sleep habits will prevent a lot of crying in the long run."

William Sears et al.: *The Baby Sleep Book*

Dr. William Sears's *The Baby Sleep Book* is the most popular example of the attachment parenting method of getting a baby to sleep. In fact, Dr. Sears is credited with coining the phrase. *Attachment parenting* is the name of a parenting philosophy that traces its origins to the attachment theory of human development that I discussed in Chapter 2.

Attachment parenting asks parents to do what they are naturally inclined to do: be sensitive to their baby's needs. It isn't clear that parents need to be reminded to do this. Although Dr. Sears allows room for parents who don't wish to breast-feed their baby every time she cries or to have the baby sleep in bed with them, his books demonstrate a clear bias in this direction.

Some critics of Dr. Sears's work point out that attachment parenting has never been empirically tested to see if children raised this way are in fact happier and healthier than other children. Others criticize his sleep recommendations for his support of bed sharing, which contradicts the recommendations of the American Academy of Pediatrics and the Consumer Product Safety Commission. Still others complain that attachment parenting places undue burdens on already stressed-out parents.

My own view of the Sears sleep book is that it does not address the problem of babies developing adverse sleep associations, as described by Ferber and others. As a baby begins to develop her own internal methods of self-soothing at around four to six months, she also develops sleep associations with what's around her when she falls asleep. If those sleep associations include the bed where her parents are sleeping (more likely trying to sleep), contact with her mother's breast, or even just contact with her mother's body, then the baby will be unable to fall asleep without these associations present. Let me be clear: If you want your baby and toddler to remain literally attached to you for the first several years of her life, then attachment parenting is a fine way to go. But don't let yourself be persuaded that your toddler will easily separate from you when you (or dad) have had enough of baby in bed.

Hundreds of parents have complained to me in my office that they cannot get their toddler out of their bed and that they wish they never gone down this road. One might argue that their distress is caused by incorrectly following attachment parenting advice, but I would argue that they probably have followed that advice too well.

The Risks of Bed Sharing

Co-sleeping is an arrangement where the baby is easily accessible next to the bed (through a device that attaches to the bed), whereas in *bed sharing* a baby sleeps with her parents in the same bed. The suggestion that solo sleeping is safer than co-sleeping cannot be supported by epidemiological data. Sharing your bed with your baby poses risks, which, though small, are measurable. And they are preventable. The 2011 AAP policy statement on bed sharing reads as follows:

> Despite a major decrease in the incidence of sudden infant death syndrome (SIDS) since the American Academy of Pediatrics (AAP) released its recommendation in 1992 that infants be placed for sleep in a nonprone position, this decline has plateaued in recent years. Concurrently, other causes of sudden unexpected infant death that occur during sleep (sleep-related deaths), including suffocation, asphyxia, and entrapment, and ill-defined or unspecified causes of death have increased in incidence, particularly since the AAP published its last statement on SIDS in 2005. It has become increasingly important to address these other causes of sleep-related infant death. Many of the modifiable and nonmodifiable risk factors for SIDS and suffocation are strikingly similar. The AAP, therefore, is expanding its recommendations from focusing only on SIDS to focusing on a safe sleep environment that can reduce the risk of all sleep-related infant deaths, including SIDS.

What the AAP statement means, in a nutshell, is this: SIDS deaths have declined dramatically since the initiation of the Back to Sleep campaign, but infant deaths in beds from preventable causes like suffocation continue to occur. The policy statement specifies ways that bed sharing poses risks to sleeping babies. Dr. Sears's response to statements such as these from the AAP is to suggest, implausibly, that bed-sharing parents should buy king-size beds.

About once a month I get a call from parents who are panicked because their baby just rolled off the bed onto the floor. Sometimes the parents don't even bother to call me; they take the baby directly to the emergency department. Accidents such as these, even if they cause no harm, are preventable and unnecessary.

I understand that bed sharing is common in other countries and has a long history in this one. Some would even say that bed sharing carries the weight of tradition, but, as I heard a college football announcer observe as the freshman class removed their clothes at the start of the fourth quarter in 14-degree weather, "Just because it's a tradition doesn't make it a good idea."

Sleep-Deprived for Seven Years

I recently had a consultation with a mother of a seven-year-old girl because, in her mother's words, her daughter was "chronically ill." The mother came alone with a stack of medical records and told me that her little girl had not gone more than two weeks without suffering from a cold, or an ear infection, or some other acute illness. She had been treated on numerous occasions with a number of antibiotics. Blood tests and X-rays from a previous extensive workup to discover why the girl was sick so often revealed that the child had no evidence of a problem with her immune system, was not allergic to anything, and, in fact, had a normally functioning body.

On closer questioning, her mother admitted to me that the girl had *never slept through the night in her life!* That's seven years without a single night of having slept even five hours straight. I asked the mother the same question in several different ways to make sure I had understood her correctly. This child had never had a good night's sleep. Another fact emerged: The girl slept in bed with her mother. There had been several unsuccessful attempts to get her to sleep in her own bed, which had been prepared for her but never slept in. I cannot prove that this girl's poor health was directly related to her lifelong absence of sleep, but I can say with confidence that her chronic fatigue was not making her healthier.

Dr. Rob's Sleep Philosophy

My own brand of go-to-sleep advice leans heavily toward the Ferber method.

- If possible, have the baby sleep in a room separate from yours.
- Eliminate adverse sleep associations (pacifier, nursing/feeding, holding the baby) between four and six months of age.
- Aim to place the baby down while she's still awake.
- Try to create a space of 15 to 30 minutes between the last feeding and the moment of sleep.

Sleep Associations

When parents tell me that their baby (four months or older) wakes up every two hours during the night, one of the first things I ask about are sleep associations. I want to know what surrounds the baby at the moment of sleep, since these are the things we want surrounding the baby when she moves into shallow sleep every two to three hours. Is the baby nursing or taking a bottle while she falls asleep? Does she have a binky in her mouth? Is she making contact with mom's or dad's body while she falls asleep?

If the answer to any of these question is yes, we probably have found why the child wakes so frequently at night. The solution is to remove the adverse association sooner rather than later. In my experience, cold-turkey removal is the only effective approach. Weaning a baby away from most adverse sleep association turns out to be more difficult than it sounds.

For example, it's notoriously difficult to wean a baby off a pacifier. As long as the binky remains in the house, the temptation to give it back to the baby for any reason is simply too strong. Nursing to sleep, on the other hand, lends itself much better to weaning because the object of the exercise is to increase the amount of time between the last feeding and the moment the child falls asleep. In practice, however, the toughest and most important step is the first one: taking the baby off the breast or the bottle before she is asleep.

To troubleshoot sleep associations, take the inventory on behalf of your baby. See what things she's surrounded by at the moment of sleep and make sure those are the things that will be there in two to three hours. If any of those things are difficult or impossible to reproduce in two to three hours, it's best to work at changing or removing them.

The three temptations

For a baby who has developed her own internal soothing mechanisms but who wakes in the middle of the night and demands attention, I recommend a strategy I call "Avoiding the Three Temptations." The temptations are going in to the baby, picking her up, and giving her something to eat.

I counsel parents that if they cannot resist the temptation to go in to see their fussy baby, they should resist the temptation to pick her up. Instead, I recommend stroking the baby's back and talking to her calmly and reassuringly. But if mom cannot resist the temptation to pick the baby up, she should resist the temptation to feed her. Instead, she should make calm sounds and gently rock the baby. But if she cannot resist the temptation to give the baby something to eat, she should not breast-feed or formula-feed the baby. Instead, she should give the baby a bottle of water. (Note: Never give pure water to a baby younger than four months of age; there's a small but measurable risk that the baby's blood may become diluted.) The baby does not want water. Since most babies are smart enough to reject less-than-enticing incentives for waking up, eventually, usually after a night or two, the baby realizes that waking up for water is not worth her while. Then the parents can work on resisting the first two temptations.

Siblings

Many of us are blessed to live in homes with multiple bedrooms, but many more of us don't live in places where there are even two bedrooms, let alone separate rooms for a baby *and* her older sibling. We're compelled to make do with the space we have. Often by necessity, the baby and even older siblings must sleep in the same room as the parents. Sometimes from the earliest ages siblings have to share rooms.

I am often asked if it's possible or even desirable to sleep-train a baby in a room where an older sibling is sleeping. After all, won't the older child's sleep be disrupted by the presence of the baby? It depends on how sound a sleeper your older child is. The only way to test this arrangement is to try it. It often goes better than you think it's going to go.

The presence of siblings also introduces another argument against bed sharing. Most bed-sharing families promise themselves that the older sibling will be out of the bed by the time baby arrives. More often than I care to comment, however, this does not occur. The toddler firmly refuses to leave and the parents find it impossible to remove her. Better not to have her sleeping in your bed in the first place.

Sleep for the Whole Family

When I troubleshoot sleep problems in my office, I'm careful to inquire about everybody's sleep habits, including both parents and siblings. If everybody is sleeping well, even if the baby is sleeping in a bouncy seat, the toddler is sleeping on the floor, and dad is sleeping on the couch, I tend to believe there is no problem in need of a solution. If, however, some or all members of the family are getting a lousy night's sleep, by definition there is a family-sleep problem.

If the sleeping problems or the sleeping location of the baby is the cause of the family-sleep problem, I recommend doing something about it. Maybe because I'm a father,

I always try to ask fathers if the sleeping arrangements are working for them. If the answer is no, I try to examine ways that the entire family can get a good night's rest. The solutions may entail enduring some pain (such as listening to the baby cry for a short time), but the long-term positives for the entire family will reward you for your efforts.

Remember that fatigued parents can't do the job of parenting as effectively as well-rested parents. Even if you believe your sacrifices are benefiting your baby, those benefits are likely short-term in nature. Over the long term, your chronic sleep deprivation can negatively affect your own mood, impair your ability to get adequate exercise, and even disrupt your digestive metabolism. Sleep is one of the three legs on which the structure of good health stands. Remove one of those legs and the whole thing topples.

Schedules

Every new mother dreams of getting her baby on a schedule. A few even claim to have achieved it. But the opposite is more likely the case: The baby puts mom on a schedule!

Babies eat when they're hungry and tend not to eat when they're not hungry. The exception is overfed babies who eat whenever the bottle or nipple is there, whether or not they just ate. Some nursing mothers can be lulled into the false impression that the baby is eating because she's hungry, not because she's colicky or she has reflux. In fact, the baby may be overeating.

Although you can't force a baby onto a schedule, you can nudge her there. With a little nudging and with proper reading of a baby's hunger cues, most babies and their mothers will fall into a schedule that ends up being more of a cooperative process than either a baby-directed or a parent-directed one.

A great way to help a baby get on a good feeding schedule is to allow her to learn the difference between night and day by simply letting daytime be light and nighttime be dark. Babies learn it naturally. As a human being capable of developing so-called circadian rhythms, a baby trains her own brain to learn that dark nighttime is the time when we sleep and daytime is when we stay awake.

The way you'll know that your baby is learning the difference between night and day is that she will begin to sleep longer stretches during the night. As a result, some babies, especially nursing babies, will start nursing more often during the day, often every one to two hours instead of every four hours. In exchange, they may sleep six hours or more at night. I am still waiting to meet a mother who says she minds sleeping more at night and nursing more during the day.

Twins/Multiples

Full disclosure statement: I am a twin. My twin sister and I are unusual for a couple reasons. First, though we were born in a well-regarded hospital in a major city, no one knew that my mother was pregnant with twins until my sister was born. I was delivered 20 minutes later. The other historical oddity is that we were both delivered in breech position. This would never happen today. In the early twenty-first century my mother would have been scheduled for a Cesarean section.

My mother was lucky to have two older daughters already at ages where they were able to help her. My sisters were eight and six at the time. Best of all for my mother, the girls were in school half the day so my mother got some measure of peace for part of the day and some assistance with diapers and bottles for the remainder of the day. At night, however, she was on her own. Fathers in the early 1960s generally did not contribute to basic child-rearing tasks, and our father was no exception.

Families with multiples rarely follow the rules of sleeping that you may read in this or other parenting books. These families end up feeding and resting their babies more in line with the strict by-the-clock method of Emmet Holt than with the baby-driven attachment theories of William Sears.

The reason for this is simple: *Parents of multiples have no choice.* They must either feed the babies when it's time to feed them, put them down for a nap when it's time for a nap, or go insane trying to feed multiples on demand. For parents of multiples, I even encourage them to keep lists of who ate when and how much, which I almost never recommend doing for parents of a single baby. Keeping good records, particularly for those brave moms who attempt to breast-feed twins, is essential.

Sometimes a twin or triplet will wake up and start crying when it isn't time for her to feed. I don't recommend ignoring this baby, but it's also not a particularly good idea to feed her and throw the feeding plan out of sync. Imagine how screwed up your schedule would become if you fed a baby out of sequence!

It is best to get a system in place for multiples as soon as possible. In practice, most parents of multiples try several iterations of a sleeping and feeding schedule before they settle on something that works. As the babies mature and their sleeping patterns change, the plan and the schedules change with them.

It's difficult, if not impossible, to care for multiples alone. It's really important for these mothers to get help. If a mother can't get the support and help from dad, either because he has to work or is otherwise indisposed, she can appeal to family members or even friends.

Napping and Nighttime

For reasons that remain mysterious, babies seem to know the difference between nap time and nighttime, and they treat each sleep experience differently. There are many babies in my practice who sleep solidly six to eight hours at night but who nap infrequently or inconsistently. As long as the baby is getting enough total sleep during a 24-hour period, inconsistent napping doesn't seem to be a problem.

Most experts will tell you, and experienced parents will confirm, however, that a baby who naps well during the day will sleep better at night. This is because the baby who naps will avoid overstimulation during the day. So what do you do if your baby is a bad napper? Since sleeping is one of those things you can't force a baby to do, I usually recommend the next best thing: downtime.

Since stimulation is the problem that disrupts nighttime sleep, I recommend that during nap time parents place the baby in a low-stimulation environment—one with low light and low sound—for at least an hour. Mom can stay near the baby so long as she turns the lights down and doesn't actively engage the baby in any kind of stimulating play.

The busy household

Sometimes creating downtime can be a challenge. Some homes, especially ones with older children, just cannot be made quiet enough or dark enough to provide a low-stimulation environment. More often the problem is not the home but the "To-Do" list. Busy moms with lots of stuff to do and lots of places to go may have difficulty finding quiet, dark locations for their young baby to sleep. These often end up being babies who don't sleep well at night because they aren't given a chance to nap well during the day.

These babies often end up napping in the car. After several hours of bouncing back and forth from place to place, being oohed and aahed over by friends, family members, and passersby, the baby takes advantage of the soothing low-pitched rumble of the engine and falls asleep. The challenge is then to transition the baby from the car to the crib without waking her up. Many mothers will tell you that this transition seldom works. It may make more sense to bring a book, magazine, or electronic device with you when you drive your baby so that you can occupy yourself while your baby sleeps in the back seat.

Sleeping in strange places

The car may not be the only place you need to let your baby sleep. Sometimes you just need to adjust your schedule to allow your baby to sleep where she is.

One summer we took our first child to a street fair when he was around nine months old. He fell asleep in his stroller, having just shared an orange with me, and his face was completely covered with orange juice and bits of pulp. He then was set upon by a contingent of bees that clearly liked the smell of oranges. None of them were angry and I wasn't concerned about his being stung, but I didn't like the idea of all those bees flying around. The problem was I couldn't shoo them away without risking waking up the boy. So I let them do their thing until they got bored and flew away. It was a bit awkward to sit in the shade with my son covered in happy, curious bees as neighbors strolled past wondering if I planned to do anything about it.

Tired mothers often seek out movie theaters, especially during hot summers, because they tend to have air conditioning that works and they are dark—perfect for napping— as long as the feature is a quiet drama and the baby doesn't wake up.

Many young parents are invited to join friends and family at church or synagogue. There are a few things to consider before taking your baby to services. Houses of worship tend to present special problems for young babies, particularly babies who are nursing. Although there are some faith communities that welcome children of all ages into a worship spaces, this is hardly universal. Most houses of worship try to maintain a solemn, prayerful atmosphere, and parents are asked respectfully to keep young children out of worship spaces. The obvious exceptions are baptisms, christenings, and baby-naming ceremonies. Some houses of worship provide child care and even private rooms for nursing. As in a movie theater, a sleeping baby during services is fine, but a crying baby would have to be taken out. It's always best to ask or call ahead to find out what kinds of accommodations are available for babies and mothers.

Troubleshooting

If your chosen sleep routine is not working, it's a good idea to return to square one and to review everything that goes on around nighttime sleeping. There may be some areas that are ripe for troubleshooting.

Overstimulation: I start by asking parents to describe their bedtime routine. I think of the bedtime routine as a series of highly predictable events that begins at your baby's dinner time and ends when she falls asleep. The time frame we are talking about may be anywhere from 30 to 60 minutes in length.

I listen particularly for indications that the baby may be overstimulated during this period. For example, is the lighting bright and harsh? Is the television on, even softly? Is there music playing? Are there a lot of people talking loudly? Is everybody passing the baby back and forth among themselves?

If it turns out that there are too many stimuli, I discuss ways to reduce them, which sometimes is more easily said than done. In some homes there are simply too many people and too much surrounding chaos to reduce stimulation. Dr. Spock would argue that this is not necessarily a bad thing and that babies will get used to it, but Dr. Weissbluth and I would not agree with him. In general, less stimulation is better than more, and the empiric research seems to corroborate this. The trick is finding a way to reduce stimuli. The solution may be to find a quiet but well-ventilated corner of the house or apartment where light, sound, and tactile stimulation can be kept to a minimum.

Teething: Teething pain often interrupts the process of getting a baby to learn to go to sleep. At around four months of age, give or take, a baby may start drooling much more than before and may start grinding her fist into her mouth. This is likely the start of the teething process, though actual teeth may not appear for eight months. I cover teething in more depth in Chapter 8.

Colic: Although I dealt with colic and remedies in more depth in Chapter 5, I mention it here because colic almost always happens when babies and their parents want to be sleeping. Once all the other causes of crying have been ruled out (baby just ate so she can't be hungry, diaper is clean, she's not constipated, and so on), you might settle on colic as the cause.

Constipation: This is actually a subcategory of colic. Many babies wake up crying because they have to poop and they can't. There are many easy ways to help a baby through constipation problems, and we'll deal with some of them in Chapter 8.

Need for more calories? In Chapter 4 I discussed a problem that often arises in babies between four and six months of age. A healthy baby that is born to a healthy mother and grows as fast a human being can grow eventually reaches the point where 20-calorie-per-ounce breast milk or formula is no longer sufficient for her needs throughout the entire day. Sometimes the baby will signal this change by waking up in the night at times when she used to sleep. This phenomenon is real but is often short-lived because feeding is so often a self-regulated phenomenon. Breast-fed babies will stimulate their mothers to make more milk during the day, and formula-fed babies will drink larger or more frequent bottles. Sometimes it works, sometimes not. I discuss introduction of solid foods as a remedy in Chapter 4.

Notes:

- How can you use context and a broad range of what's defined as "normal" to evaluate your baby's growth and development?
- What's abnormal growth and when do you need to see your pediatrician?
- What's abnormal development and when do you need to see your pediatrician?

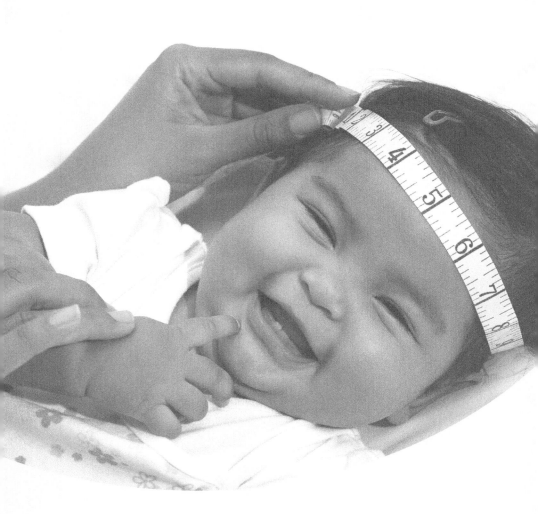

Chapter 7

Growth and Development

How often does a stranger observe your baby on the living room carpet and say, "You know? That baby is spot-on perfect"? The answer is practically never. Instead, you usually hear, "Wow! That's a *big* baby!" or "She's such a *peanut*!" Folks almost never comment on how *normal* your baby appears. That's unfortunate, because comments like these have a way of sneaking inside a parent's head and causing him or her to wonder if the stranger in the living room may be right.

Well-meaning friends and neighbors—as well as relatives, including your parents—frequently toss off comments about your baby's development that often can be frightening: "Oh, she's not rolling over yet? My friend's daughter didn't roll over at four months and she ended up having Boney Maroney Syndrome." The temptation to say such things must be irresistible because so many people do it, though if they took some time to reflect, they might think twice.

And then there are your own parents. Even more than friends and neighbors, grandparents usually mean well when they make comments about your baby's growth and development. Sometimes, however, there may be some hidden criticism in their remarks. For example, grandma's comment about how tiny your baby is may be a veiled criticism of the way you feed your baby ("I didn't breast-feed you and you turned out just fine").

You're probably already worried about how well your baby is progressing. In part to counteract the inevitable comments you'll receive on your baby's progress or lack of it, my aim in this chapter is to give you an overview based on science and my experience of baby growth and development over the first six months. I'll offer some simple, sensible guidelines for determining whether your baby falls in the "normal" range or is off the charts and whether you should consider consulting with your pediatrician.

The "Science" of Pediatrics

Human growth and development are the new *raison d'etre* of pediatrics. Pediatrics originally came into being around the turn of the twentieth century to solve two problems: infant mortality and malnutrition. By the mid-twentieth century, both problems had been solved, at least in the developed world. Pediatrics continues to exist because of its specialized body of knowledge regarding normal and abnormal growth and development.

It can be argued persuasively that the study of human growth and development is the "science" of pediatrics. For this reason, among others, we still need pediatricians. Otherwise we could probably pass the care of infants and children back to the general practitioner (now called the "family practitioner").

Of course, the term "science" is a bit self-congratulatory when applied to pediatrics. At the cellular level, development is indeed a science; it is inextricably entwined with genetics and molecular biology (there is even a top-drawer scientific journal called *Development*). When we are talking about real babies and children, however, we can only observe how they grow and develop and then decide where we will place the boundary markers that separate "normal" from "abnormal." Such decisions are less scientific than culturally determined.

Herein lies a phenomenon that plagues medicine in general and pediatrics in particular: Where do we place those boundary markers? What is "normal" when we're talking about a baby's weight, length, and head circumference? What's a "normal" age at which a baby should sit on her own, pull to stand, and walk?

Statistics provide one way to answer these questions. You can weigh a group of babies at various intervals and plot their weights on a graph. Or you can mark down the age at which each baby accomplishes a given developmental task, such as walking. The result you get will resemble a bell-shaped curve, which is typical for any factor one measures in a population. Then you look at the region at the top of the curve (where the majority of the babies fall) as the average. Every baby who falls below or above this region on the curve could be considered abnormal.

Alternatively, one could define standard measurements for given ages and standard ages for achievement of given milestones, and define any baby who fails to meet these standards as abnormal.

The current state of the science of pediatrics is a complicated mixture of these two approaches. There are well-defined ranges of normal for all growth factors and developmental milestones. Furthermore, it is known that children who fall out of the range of these factors or who fail to grow and develop at well-defined rates (either too quickly or too slowly) may be at risk for various medical problems that would benefit from a pediatrician's intervention.

Too often in the early twenty-first century, however, we have relied on target numbers and target dates and have raised red flags when they didn't need to be raised. For example, if an infant does not smile at her parents at six weeks of age, should the parents call the pediatrician and request an evaluation for autism? Without knowing anything else about the baby, the answer would be no, but this is precisely what is happening today.

In my practice, I recommend an approach to growth and development based on two fundamental principles. The first is context. By context, I mean understanding a baby's weight, head size, or developmental stage in light of the totality of the baby's life. Was she born prematurely? Are both of her parents small or large? Doesn't dad have a really big head (so we shouldn't be surprised that his baby does, too)? What about every other aspect of the baby's development? Are the other factors normal? Finally, what has the baby been doing *over time*? Has she been growing along a curve or falling off one? Has her development been progressing or has it stalled? Out of context, any so-called abnormal growth or developmental factor is meaningless.

The second fundamental principle is a bias regarding the size of the range of normal. It is an unfortunate fact of life that the range of normal in this country has been shrinking for some time. Children are not growing more quickly or more slowly than they used to, and there are not more developmentally delayed children now than in the past. What has changed is the placement of the boundary markers between normal and abnormal.

My bias is to expand the range or normal rather than to shrink it. I do this for a few reasons. First, with regard to growth factors, most babies with "abnormal" percentiles are perfectly healthy: They eat in a healthy manner and their growth and development progresses as expected. It doesn't make sense to intervene on behalf of these children because there is *nothing fundamentally wrong* with them apart from the fact that they are big or small. Second, in most cases, if a growth or developmental factor is abnormal, there is nothing that anybody can do about it. To the contrary: It is often *more harmful to intervene* than it is to watch and wait.

For example, a tiny baby born to a tiny mom (from a tiny family) is born healthy and breast-feeds like a champion. She gains weight within the acceptable range of normal but at the low end of it. In today's world, the mother of this baby may be asked to supplement her baby with formula or to start solids before her baby is ready. But doing so is more likely to disrupt the normal healthy feeding relationship that mother and baby already have than to benefit the baby. After all, she's a healthy thriving baby. Our tendency to try to fix what ain't broke may end up doing more harm than good.

Here's another example from the other end of the growth curve (a true story from my practice). A healthy ten-pound newborn also breast-feeds like a champion and gains a lot of weight. But she doesn't roll over by six months. She also doesn't pull to stand by nine months. That's because by six months she weighs twenty-one pounds! In every other aspect of her growth and development she is stone-cold normal. In today's world, this baby would be referred to an early-intervention developmental screening program. But this baby isn't developmentally delayed; she's *large*. I'll discuss later why she may appear to be developmentally delayed in the section on gross motor development.

The Value of Context and a Broad Range of Normal

When you consider context in evaluation of growth and development, and when you tend to expand rather than shrink the range of normal, a few important consequences result. First, you tend to develop respect for the diversity of human beings. You tend to nurture what political philosopher Michael Sandel refers to as "openness to the unbidden." By this, Sandel means an appreciation for the preciousness and uniqueness of each human life in contrast to an unhealthy focus on deviation from a concept of an ideal human being.

Second, and more difficult to measure, is reducing parental anxiety. We all know that parenting is an exceedingly stressful enterprise. There is enough to be anxious about in family life *without* worrying about a child's growth and development. If "fixing" a growth or developmental "problem" that is not fixable (and is not even a problem) will do more harm than good, it seems pointless and wasteful to intervene. This isn't an argument in favor of an anxiety-free utopia, only a plea to turn down the temperature in a feverishly anxious world.

Finally, on the subject of waste: Overtreatment of nonproblems is enormously wasteful of your precious time with your baby, not to mention a tax on an already overburdened health care delivery system. Virtually all grandparents look back with astonishment at how quickly their own children grew up and became parents themselves. Heaven forbid that any of that precious time should be wasted pursuing ideals of size and achievement.

With that lengthy introduction, let's take a tour of the science of human growth and development in the first six months of life.

Growth Expectations for the First Six Months of Life

By the time your pediatrician starts to weigh and measure your baby, it is likely her growth has already begun to be measured. Prenatal ultrasound technology has advanced to the extent that we can see small structures in a developing baby and assess the function of the heart and the kidneys. But for all its advantages, prenatal ultrasound remains frustratingly poor at predicting how much a baby is going to weigh at birth. I have seen ultrasounds misjudge a baby's birth weight by as much as a pound in either direction.

Despite these inaccuracies in prenatal ultrasounds, estimates of a baby's weight and rate of growth have been made before the baby is born. In many cases, doctors and parents base treatment decisions, such as whether to induce delivery or to go to Caesarean section, on ultrasounds. As a result, I meet many parents who are nervous about their baby's growth before she is even born. One of the objectives of this chapter is to reduce some of this anxiety by showing parents how to view growth and development factors through the lenses of context and a broad range of normal.

Birth to One Month: The Delta

Newborn babies lose weight. For reasons we discussed in Chapter 1, they are designed to lose weight. I don't expect a normal, exclusively breast-fed baby to achieve her birth weight until roughly two weeks of age. Many breast-fed babies reach their birth weight sooner, and a larger proportion of bottle-fed babies do as well.

The range of normal for weight gain in the first month is anywhere between one-half to two ounces a day. No matter how much a baby weighs when she is born, her place on the growth curve is not nearly as important as how much weight she gains over time. What I look for is a smooth progression of weight over time. In scientific notation the difference between two values of a factor is referred to as the "delta," for the Greek letter that is often used to symbolize a difference. What I'm interested in is the delta, not the absolute value, of the weight or of any other growth factor.

Of the three major growth factors—weight, length, and head circumference—weight is the factor that is most easily measured accurately and reproducibly. Just by observing a wriggly newborn baby, you can appreciate how difficult it is to get an accurate measurement of length.

What this means is that you may be handed a bunch of growth curves after a checkup, but weight is the only one that is truly precise and reproducible. For example, it's not unusual for us to "discover" that a baby's head has shrunk between visits. Of course this doesn't happen, but head measurement is an inexact science. Only after several months and measurements can we get a good sense of how quickly a baby is growing in length and head size.

A Tip from Dr Rob:

Measuring Head Circumference

To measure head circumference, we place a cloth or paper measuring tape around the widest part of the baby's skull. It turns out this measurement varies according to who is measuring. That is to say, depending on where the tape is placed, two different people can measure two different head circumferences. In my office, I try to have the same individual do all the head measurements on a baby over time. I've found this method affords the best chance of getting consistent placement of the tape measure and usually results in consistent, believable results.

Another word about head size: Parents virtually never ask why we measure heads, so pediatricians don't often explain why we do this. Head growth is a proxy for brain growth. An infant's brain grows more in the first year of life than during any other period. A head will not grow if the brain is not growing. We measure heads to make sure that the brain is growing as we expect.

Understanding context is crucial to making decisions based on evaluation of the baby's head. A baby with a large head who isn't developing or whose development has stalled is a lot more worrisome than a perfectly normal baby with a large head. I would be more likely to pursue further examinations on the baby whose development is not normal.

One Long Growth Spurt

Many parents ask me if I think their baby may be undergoing a growth spurt. If the baby is less than six months old, my answer is usually yes. That's because the first six months, especially the first four months, can be a period of explosive growth. It's often difficult to tell during the first four months of life where a baby will end up on a growth curve because the growth is so rapid that the baby's weight will "cross percentiles." In short, the first six months of life are one long growth spurt.

The slow grower

For some babies, however, growth is not exactly explosive. Again, to understand why one baby grows more slowly than others, it's important to look at the context. First and foremost, I always want to know from parents how well the baby is feeding. How long does she nurse? Does she "loll at the breast" or does she eat hungrily and fall asleep? How often does she feed? If she's bottle-fed, how many ounces does she take and how often? (For formula-fed babies who don't gain weight, I also confirm with parents that the formula is being prepared correctly.) Finally, and perhaps most importantly: Is the baby gaining weight but losing percentiles? (I talk about percentiles more below.) Is she losing weight? If the answer to either of the last two questions is yes, I'm much more likely to pursue the matter further.

One key in the evaluation of the slow grower is head circumference. If, for whatever reason, the baby isn't getting enough calories to gain weight, the baby's head will nevertheless continue to grow normally. That is because the baby's body somehow knows that brain growth is so critically important that most of the calories dedicated to growth go to the brain before they go to any other part of the body. If the baby's head is also not growing, I suspect another difficulty, such as a problem with metabolism. At this point, I'm likely to obtain blood tests and/or to refer the baby to a specialist.

Pursuing the matter of slow growth further may involve seeking the help of a lactation consultant. And for babies with particular trouble gaining weight, sometimes frequent weight checks are all we need to do to reassure mom (and the pediatrician) that the baby is feeding well.

Two easy rules of thumb

Rather than focusing on the minutia of your baby's weight gain, it's useful to keep in mind two easy-to-remember guidelines: Your baby is likely to double her birth weight by six months of life and to triple it by one year. For example, a 7-pound, 8-ounce newborn is likely to weigh more or less 15 pounds at six months and 22 pounds, 8 ounces at her first birthday. For some preemies, it's more accurate to use their weight at their expected birthday. Many premature infants grow slowly, at least at first, so for them this guideline may not work.

At all times, however, what matters most to me as a pediatrician is not what a baby weighs at any given age but rather what the baby is eating and how well she is eating it. *Healthy feeding, not weight, is the single most important indicator of a baby's health.* It turns out that if a baby eats well, weight gain takes care of itself. If a baby appears to eat well but doesn't gain weight *over time* (focusing on the delta), then I investigate further.

Developmental Expectations during the First Six Months

Regarding developmental milestones, an understanding of the breadth of the range of normal as well as an appreciation of context becomes important. Infant development is usually divided into three parts: gross motor (movements of the head and limbs), fine motor (movements of the fingers and mouth), and social-cognitive (encompassing what the baby "knows" and how she interacts with the world, including "talking"). It's important to realize that these three phases of development do not always advance at the same rate. I recommend appreciating the advance of one aspect of a baby's development in context with the other phases. For example, if a six-month-old baby laughs, coos, and responds to her mother's facial expressions, and if she supports her weight on her legs and "tripod" sits, I'm not so concerned if she doesn't yet roll over.

Because the range of normal is so broad, I've included on this list the things that most babies can do by a certain age rather than what the average baby can do or what the super-advanced baby can do. Keep in mind when perusing this list that any single factor is not as important as the broad overview of what a baby can do at any age.

	Gross motor	Fine motor	Social-cognitive
1 month	lifts head briefly when lying on stomach	"iron grip," strong suck	stares at faces
2 months	holds head up for brief periods	loses "iron grip" and other infantile reflexes	coos, smiles reflexively
4 months	good head control, often brings hands to mouth	grasps toys	smiles easily
6 months	bears weight on legs, can sit when supported	coordinated enough for solid foods	engages in "nonsense" conversations

More on gross motor milestones

Gross motor development, just like physical development in general, has three parts: size, strength, and coordination. These three factors do not advance at the same rate.

Take our example of the six-month-old, 21-pound baby girl who doesn't roll over. This baby may be strong enough to roll over, and she may be coordinated enough to roll over, but her healthy, 21-pound body may be too large for her to turn it over.

On another spot in the spectrum, we have a one-month-old skinny baby who rolls over all the time, but not because she wants to. She may not have much muscular strength, and we don't expect her to have much coordination at all, but she flips over all the time because she is long and lanky and small movements of her arms cause her to turn over. This baby is probably as surprised as her parents that she rolls over and probably is frightened by the sudden change in perspective. Often babies like this one actually *lose* the ability to roll over before they regain it simply by virtue of the fact that they gain enough weight between one and six months that they have to wait for their strength and coordination to catch up before they can roll over again.

Another example is the unusually tall, slender, six-month-old who doesn't sit up well on her own. She has plenty of strength and she's certainly not too heavy. She simply is not yet coordinated enough to balance all that body over her center of gravity and to keep it there without falling over.

In all three of these examples, with careful watching and waiting, size, strength, and coordination all catch up to one another, and all these babies achieve their developmental milestones.

More on fine motor milestones

Apart from her ability to grasp and to suck, there aren't many fine motor skills that an infant needs during the first six months of life. This is because these babies aren't feeding themselves so purposeful movements aren't very important for their daily activities, which mostly involve eating and sleeping. An exception to this rule are the muscles of the face, particularly those of the mouth. At birth, a full-term baby should have a fully developed latch-and-suck reflex. If she didn't, she wouldn't be able to nurse. For this reason, many premature babies aren't able to feed themselves adequately and may need to be tube-fed in a special-care nursery. Generally by 40 weeks gestation, and usually earlier than this, a baby can suck and swallow in a coordinated fashion. By four months of age, a baby is coordinated enough to use her tongue to take a semisolid blob from the front to the back of the mouth and swallow it. This is why many four-month-olds can handle solid foods.

More on social-cognitive development

In this age of early detection of pervasive developmental disorders of which autism is the exemplar, much is made of the development of the social smile. I admit that I, too, anxiously awaited the appearance of the first social smile on our first baby. As with any other developmental milestone, the social smile ought to be understood in context. For example, a premature baby wouldn't be expected to smile at six weeks of age if she were born five weeks early.

Equally important as the smile is a baby's interest in faces. Even without smiling, the gaze of a one-month-old baby is often drawn to faces more than to shapes. No one knows why this is the case, but it is compelling to wave one's hand and simply say that the propensity to look at faces is "hard-wired" into the human brain. This is a good thing, because we are thereby primed to learn to relate to other human beings practically from birth. And because the mouth is conveniently located on the face, an infant is primed to focus on the organ of speech, which she will soon try to imitate by cooing and verbalizing.

By around six months of age, a baby becomes sensitive to the expression on a caregiver's face. If you smile at her, she will smile back and may even laugh. If you furrow your brow, the baby may become anxious and cry. Often I have to remind myself during an office visit to always smile and speak in a pleasant tone of voice when there is a six-month-old in the room, regardless of the seriousness of the discussion. If I wrinkle my brow in concentration or start to speak too loudly, the baby may interpret that I am angry and she may react by starting to cry. Keeping my expression and tone of voice in mind is good policy but difficult to implement in practice. Fortunately for most parents, it's easy to be happy around six-month-olds.

What Do Percentiles Mean?

Whenever you study a large group of people and compare some measurement such as weight or height, the results you get resemble a bell-shaped curve. This is simply a feature of the normal distribution of any continuous set of values. From these curves, it's pretty simple to spot the average, or mean: It's the peak of the bell curve. We call the average the 50th percentile, because half the individuals fall above this point and half fall below it. One can then measure how many individuals are in the regions close to the 50th percentile and how many are in the regions farther away. For example, at the 75th percentile for weight we can say that three-quarters of individuals will weigh less and one-quarter will weigh more. For another example, at the 25th percentile for height we can say that three out of four babies are longer and one out of four is shorter.

A problem in interpretation occurs when a baby falls above the 99th percentile or below the 1st percentile. I once had a mother of a 99++% tall baby ask me, "So Dr. Rob, are you saying my baby doesn't exist?" (She was kidding, of course.) The answer is that these bell-shaped curves have long tails on both the low and the high ends. There will always be individuals who seem to be statistically impossibly tall or short, heavy or light. It merits repeating here that a baby's place on or off the growth curve is not nearly as important as the rate of her growth.

Another problem with our growth curves is that they are standardized for full-term, American babies. Premature babies will lag behind full-term babies, sometimes for considerable periods. There are some published "preemie growth curves" that take a baby's gestational age into account. I never use these charts precisely because the place on the curve never matters as much as the delta. There are also specialized curves for children born with certain well-known conditions such as Down syndrome. These curves are generally only useful for specialists.

How to Tell if There Are Any Problems with Growth or Development

Keep in mind that an individual point on a growth curve is almost meaningless. An informed interpretation of the meaning of that point takes into account all the points that come before it and other information about the baby (for instance, whether the baby is a preemie and whether she has any underlying conditions).

Too little growth

In my office, if measurement of height, weight, or head circumference is suddenly lower or higher than we expect based on the baby's prior growth, we repeat the measurement. Babies don't shrink. If a baby is suddenly shorter than she was two months ago, we remeasure. Sometimes we find that our current measurement was off or that a previous measurement must have been wrong.

One measurement that is almost never wrong is weight. If a baby suddenly loses weight, I want to know why. Or if the baby has been gradually drifting down from her normal place on the growth curve, I begin to ask why. These are babies who are not actually losing weight over an extended period, but who are gaining weight more slowly than expected.

Any change in body weight over time can be described by a subtraction equation: what goes into a baby in the form of calories eaten minus what comes out in terms of calories burned. If you consume more calories than you burn over a given period of time, you gain weight. Conversely, you lose weight if you burn more calories than you consume over a given period. There are a couple of common explanations for why a baby would gain weight more slowly than expected. Most commonly, the baby is becoming more active. After four months of age, and especially after six months, babies become much more mobile and they burn more calories per day. After all, when they sit happily in their bouncy seats enjoying the world, they aren't burning many calories at all. When they begin to venture out to explore their world, they may eat the same amount but may burn more calories than before. As a result, the rate of weight gain on the growth curve slows.

Another reason why the rate of weight gain may be slowing is that the baby isn't taking in enough calories to maintain normal growth. For this reason, when a baby is losing percentiles, I always ask what the baby is eating and how much. I ask about the baby's physical activity as well. Sometimes the drop in percentiles is a sign that it's time for an exclusively milk-fed baby to start solids.

As I've mentioned several times earlier, *context* matters. I also look at length and head circumference. If weight is the only growth factor that is falling off course, it's a lot less concerning than if all three are drifting downward. The size of the parents and their own growth history as babies also needs to be taken into account.

Too much growth

It's more common in my practice to encounter babies who seem to accelerate up growth percentiles rather than down them. This is especially true of weight. If a baby is gaining weight abnormally quickly, the first question is usually, "What is the baby eating, and how much?" If the baby is exclusively breast-fed, there usually isn't a problem: The baby is simply healthy and is growing quickly. The situation is somewhat different for formula-fed babies: They may be overeating. After glancing at the growth curves, I make sure to ask the caregiver how much the baby is eating and how often. Sometimes I learn that mom is "spiking" the formula with cereal. This affords me the opportunity to discuss healthy feeding practices for babies.

Heads

Sometimes heads grow more quickly than we expect them to. Although it's unlikely that a baby's brain would grow too quickly, sometimes the fluid spaces in the brain and surrounding the brain expand more quickly than expected. This is one of the many instances when understanding context is crucial to making decisions regarding evaluation of the baby's head. Is the baby developing normally? Does dad or mom have a big head? If mom or dad (or both) has a large head, then it stands to reason that their baby's head might be larger than average. If there is no good explanation for a baby with a large head, or if the baby is not developing as expected, I tend to investigate further. Likewise, if the head isn't growing *quickly enough* while the rest of the baby is growing well, further investigation may be necessary.

The shape of the baby's head is as important, if not more important, than overall head size. I examine a baby's head to make sure that the shape is more or less oval. Some peculiarities of head growth deserve mention here. The highly successful Back to Sleep campaign to reduce SIDS has had one unintended consequence. All those babies sleeping on their backs has resulted in an increase in "positional plagiocephaly," or, more commonly, "flat head." As many as 10% of babies who sleep only on their backs will have at least some degree of flattening, which may affect the measurement of head circumference. Flat head is a fairly benign condition. Most baby heads begin to adopt the more usual oval conformation once the baby begins rolling over at four to six months. The major difficulty a baby with a flat head may encounter is that her neck may become stiff from facing in the same direction for a long period. I refer these babies to physical therapy, where the problem usually resolves quickly.

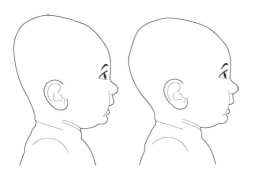

Positional plagiocephaly (left) is an abnormal flattening of the back of the head that can occur if the baby sleeps largely on her back. It has become more common since parents have preferentially put their babies to sleep on their backs to avoid SIDS. Once the baby starts rolling over (typically by six months), the skull usually takes on a rounder shape (right).

Another feature of the head that parents seem to pay a lot of attention to is the *anterior fontanelle,* commonly known as the "soft spot." The soft spot is one of the openings between the bony plates in the skull that allow a growing brain to expand. Typically, the bones are almost closed up by nine months of age. If a head isn't growing as expected, either too little or too much, I often check to see if the fontanelle is closing too early or is too wide open. In either case, more investigation is necessary, involving radiographic images of the head and/or a second opinion from a specialist in the bones of the head.

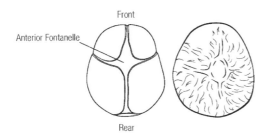

The anterior fontanelle, or "soft spot," on the top front of an infant's head is the space between the bony plates that make up the skull (left), which allows the brain to grow and is visible and palpable (right). Typically these plates close at about nine months.

Development

There are several ways to determine if a baby's development is falling within the range of normal. First, I ask parents if they have any concerns about how their baby is progressing. In my office, we give the parents a questionnaire to fill in their concerns if they have any. Most of the time I can address these concerns by asking some questions about what the baby is doing and listening to the parents' answers. Equally important is observing the baby. Often an experienced caregiver or health care provider can learn a lot about a baby's development simply by observation.

If a baby isn't doing something that the parents expect, or that the Internet or baby books say she should be doing, the first thing I look at is context. How are the other aspects of the baby's development progressing? Is she eating and growing well? If the baby is absolutely on track except for a single developmental milestone, I'm much less concerned than if she isn't eating and growing well or if she missed more than one milestone. Sometimes a baby's size can interfere with development of certain motor milestones. Really big babies may have difficulty rolling over or sitting up, for obvious reasons. Tall, skinny babies may have difficulty sitting up hands free because they can't balance their long torsos above their centers of gravity.

At any given well-baby visit, if a baby hasn't reached a milestone that we expect for that age (for example, pulling to stand at nine months of age), I frequently do not pursue it further unless there are other unusual aspects to the baby's development; for instance, if the same nine-month-old also is not vocalizing or reaching purposefully for objects. If the baby is otherwise normal but isn't pulling to a stand at twelve months, I may pursue the matter further. My rule of thumb is that I look more deeply into the problem if a baby isn't doing what we expect *two* visits after she would normally be doing it.

"Pursuing the matter further" most often means obtaining a consult from Early Intervention. Most states provide the services of physical, occupational, and speech therapists who evaluate the development of babies and children. If, as a result of these evaluations, the therapists determine that the baby is truly behind in her development, they will begin a program designed to help the baby catch up. Early Intervention programs have enjoyed enormous success. In my experience, if an Early Intervention team believes that a baby's delays require more investigation, they will suggest a referral to a specialist.

The Value of Watchful Waiting

A baby in my practice concerned her parents because she had not smiled at them by the time of her two-month well-baby visit. This baby had been born full-term, 7½ pounds, 20 inches, with a 14-inch head circumference. She was exclusively breast-fed and regained her birth weight by one week of age. At one month, she had grown an inch and a half and gained almost two pounds, she was waking every two to three hours to feed, and she was peeing and pooping many times per day.

By two months of age, the baby could fix her gaze on her parents' faces and could follow them as they walked across the room. She stared at her black-and-white mobile and waved her arms around as it spun. The only thing she didn't do was smile.

I counseled these parents to watch and wait: The baby's development was spot-on in every respect except the lateness of the smile. She seemed interactive. She connected with faces and objects in her world. I predicted that this baby would smile soon.

Sure enough, when I saw the baby at four months of age, she smiled back at me as soon as I made eye contact and smiled at her. The parents were relieved to hear that their baby was normal developmentally, and they were happy they had just enjoyed their new baby rather than subjecting the whole family to a stressful evaluation.

Dealing with Family, Friends, and Neighbors

No matter what you hear about how others think your baby is progressing—and you likely will hear a lot from family, friends, and neighbors—it's important to remind yourself that you're the mom now and you know your baby better than anyone else. Nevertheless, if you have doubts about your baby's growth and development, ask the pediatrician. Sometimes it's best to obtain the opinion of someone who is not as emotionally involved as family members.

The pediatrician pays attention to the context, and it's just as important that you to pay attention to the context. How is your baby feeding? Does she sleep well? Does she smile and interact with you? It's important to focus on the big picture: Is your baby happy and healthy?

Comparisons with Other Kids: Trying to Avoid the Unavoidable

Even if there were no family, friends, and neighbors to worry you about your baby's growth and development, you still might be tempted to compare your baby to other babies. It's almost inevitable: Somewhere out there is a baby that is bigger or longer than your baby. Some baby will be sitting up or rolling over before yours. Somebody's baby will be cooing and laughing before your baby does. And it may occur to you, as it occurs to every parent, that perhaps there's something wrong with your baby if she's not doing what that other baby is doing. Or perhaps you worry that you're not feeding your baby enough because that other baby is so much bigger.

When you're troubled by doubts like this, try to remind yourself of a few things. Your baby is unique, unlike any other human being who has ever lived. Also remember that your baby is an essentially healthy person. That is to say, it is an element of her essence that she is normal. There may be things about her that aren't the same as other babies but more often than not these are irrelevant. Enjoy your baby and try to appreciate what a wonderful, unique gift she is, whatever size she is and no matter what she does (or doesn't do).

- What are the signs of serious illness in your baby?
- What are the myths and facts about fever and how to treat it?
- What are the symptoms and recommended treatments for common baby illnesses?

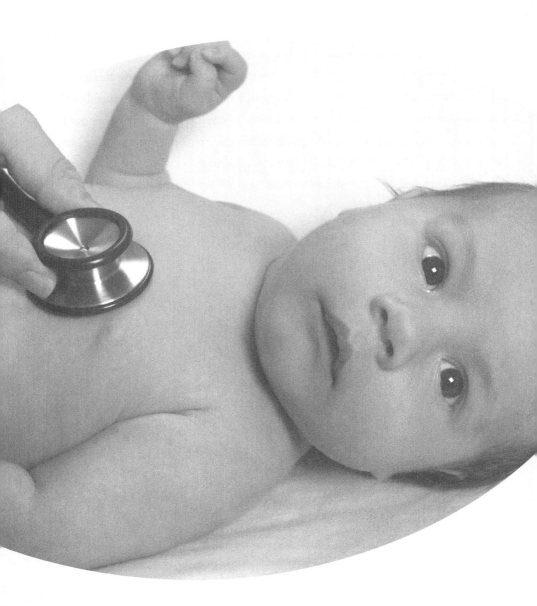

Chapter 8

Keeping Baby Healthy

Keeping a baby healthy is relatively easy. The most important things a baby needs to do are eat and sleep. If you've read the book to this point, you know pretty much all you need to know about how to keep your baby healthy. The next objective, which is even easier than feeding your baby and getting her to sleep, is helping her to keep from getting sick. For the majority of illnesses that parents need to worry about, this means keeping sick people away from the baby.

Common Infant Health Concerns and Problems

Parents who contact me with concerns during the first six months of a baby's life may not realize it, but 99% of the calls and emails I get are about the same six concerns: fever, teething, reflux, rashes, constipation, and conjunctivitis. Of these, the one that worries parents the most is fever. This is understandable. Throughout the world and across cultures, fever carries with it a portent that something dire and terrible is going to happen to the baby.

Fortunately, this is rarely true. In fact, serious illness in an otherwise healthy newborn is vanishingly rare, yet it's normal for parents to worry about their baby. This worry is also shared throughout the world and across cultures. It is my job as a pediatrician to educate families about the signs of serious illness, the symptoms that matter the most, and when to seek medical attention, even if it's only a phone call to the doctor. The aim of this chapter is to lay down some of the basics of illness in babies and how to care for a sick baby.

The Basics: What's Important to Focus On

There's one basic point to remember before moving on: the baby's feeding. When parents call me about a sick baby, I always ask how well the baby is feeding. How well the baby feeds is the single most reliable indicator of her wellness.

For example, if a mother calls me and tells me her baby has a rectal temperature of 99.9°F, but it turns out that the baby is nursing even more than normal, that's a good sign that the baby might not be all that sick. If a mother calls me and tells me that her eight-week-old hasn't nursed at all in the last twelve hours, but her rectal temperature is 98.6°F, I worry a *lot*. The point is that body temperature is not always a good indicator of how ill a baby is. There are exceptions to this rule that I'll discuss later. What's more important than temperature for most babies is how the baby appears, how she's behaving, whether she's smiling or not, and, most of all, how well she's *feeding*.

What else besides feeding?

The baby's appearance can tell you a lot about how ill a baby is. Does your baby have a strong, passionate cry, or is it weak and miserable? Is her skin warm and pink, or is she cold, pasty, and dehydrated? If she's at an age where she can make eye contact with you, does she meet your gaze, or is she unable to fix her gaze and focus on anything?

The baby's smile is another key sign of her wellness or the absence of a serious illness. A baby who smiles may be sick but she is very likely not SICK. (One of the important tasks in a pediatrics residency is to learn the difference between sick and SICK. My job as a pediatrician is to teach *you* how to tell the difference.) Just as with feeding, if a baby is smiling, it's a lot less worrisome than if a baby who used to smile all day has stopped smiling at all.

Once a baby reaches four months, she becomes playful, even if her play consists only of doing the "happy dance." A baby who is sick but who still wants to play is not as worrisome as a baby who doesn't appear sick but abruptly suspends her usual playful activities.

What goes in vs. what comes out

I get a lot of phone calls about babies who are vomiting, have diarrhea, or both. It's natural for parents to worry when their baby seems to be throwing up everything she eats or losing more into her diaper than she takes in by mouth. I always check with the parents about how well the baby is eating, by which I mean how well she is taking fluids. A six-month-old who has started solids may stop eating when she becomes ill, but she shouldn't stop drinking. Remember that a person can go days without eating food, but no one can last even a day without drinking fluids.

It's much more important to focus on what goes into your baby in the form of fluids than on what she throws up or loses into her diaper. "But doctor," I hear you reply, "if she loses more fluid than she takes in, won't she become dehydrated?"

It depends. It turns out that if a baby continues to drink even half of her usual intake, she most likely will recover from her illness without becoming seriously dehydrated. The signs of serious dehydration are not so subtle that you're likely to miss them: The child's mouth gets dry, her eyes become sunken, her skin loses its elasticity, and her diaper, of course, is dry. And, paradoxically, the seriously dehydrated baby loses interest in drinking.

That is why I focus on fluids. If a baby continues to take in fluids, I don't worry that she will become seriously dehydrated. In most stomach-bug illnesses that babies in North America catch, parents can stave off dehydration in their babies by keeping the fluids going in—no matter whether they come back out right away and no matter from which end they exit.

When it comes to fluid intake, what is true of stomach bugs is equally true of any other illness, especially illnesses that cause the baby to have a fever. If the baby is drinking an adequate amount of fluid, I'm a lot less worried than if the baby isn't drinking at all.

Fever: How and When to Take a Baby's Temperature

Fever in babies scares parents. The reasons for the fear are various and many of them are historical. In the past, fever often meant that the baby would not survive. In the era before vaccines, antibiotics, and safe drinking water, this unfortunately was true, and historical memory is long. Today, babies can be immunized against the historically deadly diseases of childhood, antibiotics can cure most serious bacterial infections, and there is no longer a risk of epidemic diarrheal illness. Despite all these advances, however, parents still worry about fever in their children.

The aim of this section is to help you understand the relationship of fever to illness, when to give which medications and how often, and when to seek medical attention. The most important decision points are drawn based on a baby's age. In general, the younger the baby, the more precautions we take.

What's a fever?

The designation of the word "fever" to a given core body temperature is somewhat arbitrary. The normal body temperature, 98.6°F, is somewhat arbitrary as well. Since normal individuals may have slightly higher or lower body temperatures, elevated body temperatures also vary from person to person.

Fever itself is not an illness; it is a response that we have evolved (or with which we were created, if you prefer) to help us fight off infections. Our immune system identifies foreign invaders and activates a cascade of signals that triggers the brain (specifically the hypothalamus) to raise body temperature. It turns out that most of the invading organisms that threaten us fare very poorly in hot environments. So fever is a trick our body uses to help disarm the bugs while our immune system destroys them.

We assign the name "fever" to a core body temperature of 100.4°F or higher. It's obviously not a round number in Fahrenheit, but in Centigrade it's 38° even. That is perhaps why we have drawn the line at 100.4°F. There is a higher risk of more serious illness in certain age groups, particularly the youngest babies, when the body temperature reaches 100.4°F or 38°C.

Fever myths

In medicine, there is science and there is "lore"—unscientific yet unquestioned "knowledge" passed from one generation to the next. Unfortunately, a large number of myths about fever fit more comfortably into the category of lore than of science. This would not be a problem if these myths didn't cause parents to panic and sometimes to expose their children to dangers such as alcohol baths (more on this later). This section will sort fact from fiction for some of the more popular fever myths.

Here are some of the most common myths about fever and the corrections to those myths:

- **Left untreated, body temperature will rise indefinitely.** The truth is that body temperature rises and falls *if you do nothing at all*. Appropriate doses of fever reducer will bring down a fever by 2°F at most. That is to say, acetaminophen (Tylenol) or ibuprofen (Motrin, Advil) will lower the temperature two degrees from what it would be without the medicine. Nevertheless, these can be two important degrees, and the baby may feel much better for having the medicine in her system. It's important to realize that fever reducers do not prevent body temperature from rising. Parents ought not to panic when they give a fever reducer and the baby's temperature rises. This is normal.

The Chewing Gum Myth

When I was growing up in New Jersey in the 1960s, a common piece of lore stated that if you swallowed your chewing gum it would remain in your stomach for seven years. Everybody "knew" this "fact," so I never challenged it. There was no reason to: It must be true because everybody says it's true. I've polled parents in my practice over the years and have been delighted to discover that the chewing gum myth still exists in various forms to this day, though the number of years the gum remains in the gut varies from three to ten years. This gives me an appreciation of the power and durability of lore in our culture.

- **High fever will damage or destroy your baby's brain.** The truth is that the body is incapable of producing a body temperature so high that the baby's brain, or any part of the baby's body for that matter, could be adversely affected. Remember that fever is a response that our body uses to fight infections. It never turns against us to harm us.

- **Fever means your baby has a bacterial infection and must have antibiotics.** Most fevers are caused by viral infections. Antibiotics do not help at all in viral infections and are more likely to do harm than to help. In newborns, however, the risk of serious bacterial infection outweighs the risks associated with giving antibiotics (for more, see the section below on newborns).

- **The higher the fever, the more likely your baby is to have a serious illness.** Much more important than magnitude of the fever is how the baby *looks*. An infant with a 103°F fever who eats and smiles and interacts appropriately with her parents is a lot less worrisome than an infant with a temperature of 98.6°F who stares listlessly into space and won't eat.

- **High fever will give your baby a convulsion or seizure.** The subject of seizures with fever is beyond the scope of this book, since this common (though frightening) phenomenon is not seen in babies younger than six months old. If a small baby with a fever has a seizure, it is more likely because the baby has meningitis. For our purposes, it is enough to say that it is not the fever that gave the baby the seizure, but rather the illness. For those older babies, it is not the height of the fever that causes the baby to seize, but rather the speed with which the temperature rises. Roughly 1 in 25 babies has a tendency to develop fevers rapidly and therefore is more likely to develop seizures with fever. As horrifying as these are to witness, these seizures do not cause long-term damage to the baby.

Newborns

For newborns (babies less than two months old), any core body temperature 100.4°F or higher might indicate a serious bacterial infection, such as pneumonia or meningitis. This does not mean that every newborn with a fever definitely *has* a serious bacterial infection, only that the chances are high enough (5% in an otherwise healthy baby) that taking precautions against the possibility is the wisest choice. Parents of newborns with fevers 100.4°F or higher should call their pediatrician immediately because the baby should be brought to an emergency department. There she will probably have blood and urine tests and possibly a test of the spinal fluid as well. While waiting for 48 hours for the test results, the baby will likely be treated with antibiotics until it is determined that no bacteria are growing in any of these body fluids. As scary as all these tests and treatments sound, it is worth the risk at such a young age.

Infants two to six months old

Feverish babies older than two months who have had their first round of antibacterial vaccines (see Chapter 9) are at much less risk of serious bacterial infections than newborns are. This is especially true if the baby shows some symptoms—for instance, cold or stomach-bug symptoms. For babies with fevers without any obvious signs of illness, it's important to focus on how the baby is drinking and behaving. When in doubt, contact your pediatrician and ask what you ought to do. Remember that a two-to-six-month-old with an obvious source for her fever usually does not require painful and invasive testing to figure out why she has a fever. If you have any questions, ask your pediatrician.

Taking a temperature

In general, my advice to parents is to take their baby's temperature rarely or never. In fully immunized babies older than six months of age, the recommendation is a solid *never*. In young infants, especially younger than two months of age, if the baby feels hot (not warm, but *hot*) or if the baby suddenly stops eating well for no apparent reason, then it would be a good idea to take the baby's temperature.

If your baby is sneezing but is eating well and doesn't feel hot, there's no reason to take her temperature. If your baby stops eating for 12 hours and doesn't look well, but you take the temperature and it's normal, you should *still* call the doctor.

Of the several types of thermometers on the market today, I recommend only the rectal thermometer. There are ear thermometers, skin thermometers, and pacifier thermometers. All these devices share the same feature: They don't measure the baby's true core body temperature, the only temperature that matters. The best kind of thermometer to use is the digital electronic thermometer, the kind that beeps when it reads the final temperature. Many parents use this thermometer by placing it under the baby's arm, essentially in the armpit. I do not recommend this. More often than not you end up taking the temperature of the bedding under your baby rather than the temperature of your baby herself. If you truly want to know your baby's temperature, you should take a rectal temperature. Here's how.

Use a small amount of Vaseline on the tip of the thermometer and insert it in the baby's anus not more than half an inch. In a few seconds the thermometer will beep and you can remove it and read it. Taking a temperature this way does not hurt your baby and nothing bad will happen if you do it. You will get an accurate reading of your baby's temperature.

What to give for fever

For babies younger than six months of age, there is only one acceptable medication for fever: acetaminophen, frequently available as the familiar brand Tylenol. As with any medication, you should give acetaminophen in doses appropriate for your baby's weight. The recommended interval is every four hours. Keep in mind that if you give your baby the medication as her temperature is rising, acetaminophen will not prevent this rise. It will only dial down the ultimate peak temperature by 2°F. You may have read that giving Tylenol increases the risk of asthma. In my view, this is not true. When given in recommended doses—as below—Tylenol is safe and effective.

Acetaminophen (Tylenol) Dosing Chart

Weight (lbs)	Infant drops 80 mg/0.8 ml	Children's Suspension 160 mg/5 ml
6–11 lbs	0.4 ml	1.25 ml
12–17 lbs	0.8 ml	2.5 ml
18–23 lbs	1.2 ml	3.75 ml

Dress the baby coolly and make sure she is getting plenty of fluids. I find that a well-hydrated baby does not require medication as often as a baby who doesn't drink well. Also remember that a sick baby doesn't have to eat solids. To the contrary: I don't want a baby who has started solids to compromise her fluid intake while she's ill. She needs extra fluids.

I do not recommend bathing to bring down a baby's fever. More often than not, exposing a hot baby to a tepid bath ends up being more of a shock than a benefit to the baby's system. Bathe the baby for two reasons only: because she's dirty and because she likes it.

Under no circumstances should you bathe a feverish baby with alcohol to bring down her temperature. This is a dangerous, even potentially deadly treatment. Rubbing alcohol is a poison that is easily absorbed through a baby's skin. It surprises and dismays me that this practice continues in the twenty-first century.

Common Illnesses in Babies

Most of the illnesses that your baby can catch are very common and are best treated by Drs. Mom and Dad. I mean this seriously: Both of you are not *as well* equipped to handle common illnesses as your pediatrician, you are *better* equipped to do so! Going to the doctor is too often a way to end up with a virus caught in the waiting room that your baby didn't already have and, possibly, with a prescription for a medicine that your baby may not need!

The common cold

There are estimated to be hundreds of viruses that cause the common cold, and the odds that your baby will catch at least one before age two is virtually 100%. These viruses are usually spread by contact—that is, by touching—although less often they may spread from person to person by direct coughing or sneezing. Contrary to popular belief, people *can* develop a fever with a cold, and babies are no exception. In babies, the fever usually lasts no more than four days and most often lasts less than 48 hours.

The biggest difficulty babies encounter with colds arises from all the mucus stuck in their noses. This is because babies cannot do the two things that adults can do to get relief from mucus: blow the nose and clear the throat. As a cold virus starts to clear from a baby, the mucus problem actually gets worse rather than better because the mucus gets thicker, stickier, and more difficult for the baby to move by coughing or sneezing. This is where a parent can really help a baby by sucking the mucus out of the nose using a bulb syringe or an oral suction device (such as the NoseFrida).

The cough will likely sound worse before it sounds better because of the thickness and stickiness of the mucus. This is why I get calls from parents in the latter stages of a baby's cold more often than in the early stages. The parents typically tell me that the cough sounds and feels as though it has gone into the baby's chest. This is rarely the case. Because a baby's body is small and elastic, the sounds that she generates in her nose and the back of her throat are transmitted easily into her chest. If the baby is eating and behaving well, this is usually an indication that the cough has not traveled to the lungs. The only way to be sure, though, is to listen to the baby's breathing with a stethoscope. Sometimes an office visit is necessary to allay a parent's fears.

Colds themselves usually last about four to five days. The baby could pass the cold to someone else, particularly another baby, during the first 24 to 48 hours, but the symptoms related to mucus, and sometimes the cough too, can last as long as four weeks. The "long tail" of cold symptoms means that often, particularly with babies in out-of-home daycare during the winter, a baby catches another cold before becoming completely clear of mucus. This gives parents the impression that their baby is constantly sick throughout the winter when in fact she is merely "serially sick." That clarification often comes as small comfort to parents, in my experience, but it is a fact of life in daycare.

Isn't it good to get sick?

No, actually, it's not. Many parents believe incorrectly that a baby needs to get sick during infancy to build up her immune system. The truth is that the baby is born with a fully equipped and potent immune system (see Chapter 9) that needs no assistance from respiratory viruses to do its job. Furthermore, there are so many respiratory viruses that there is no possible way that a baby could catch enough of them to become immune to the common cold. Even if she caught a different virus every two weeks starting at four months of age (when many babies enter daycare), she would not catch her last respiratory virus until she is a *sophomore in college.*

So, if at all possible, try to avoid exposure to respiratory viruses. If you're planning to place your baby in a daycare environment, exposure to viruses is a near certainty and parents will have to anticipate many sleepless nights with a baby who has a cold. And they cannot anticipate being rewarded with a baby with a stronger immune system. It turns out that smaller is better when it comes to daycare centers.

A Tip from Dr Rob:

Avoiding the Perpetual Germ Cycle at Daycare

If you must place your baby in out-of-home daycare, try to find a situation in which your baby is one of four or fewer babies. Five babies seems to be the magic number at which at least one virus circulates among the group for the entire winter.

Bronchiolitis

Bronchiolitis is a viral infection of the lungs brought on by one of several viruses that cause the common cold. Only babies are affected, mostly because of their diminutive size and their relative inability to handle all the mucus that these viruses produce. Babies with bronchiolitis have more difficulty breathing than babies with the common cold and therefore can have more difficulty eating and breathing at the same time. They sometimes use extra muscles in their belly, ribs, and neck to help themselves breathe, and the noise they make when they breathe sounds like the agitator of an old-fashioned washing machine.

Most babies with bronchiolitis do well and manage to eat and breathe at the same time. Some, however, become sicker and need hospitalization where oxygen and IV fluids can help them while they get over the virus on their own. If you have any concerns that your baby with bronchiolitis is not doing well, I recommend contacting your pediatrician without delay.

Ear infections

The middle ear infection is the bogeyman of pediatrics. For the most part, the general population misunderstands middle ear infections; everyone is afraid of them, usually without good reason. For example, most people don't know that roughly 80% of acute bacterial ear infections resolve on their own without antibiotic treatment. Furthermore, most people don't know that the risk-benefit calculation for using antibiotics in ear infections suggests that the therapy is more likely to harm the child than to help with her symptoms. Nevertheless, one of the more common reasons why parents seek my attention in the office is the fear of ear infections.

A bacterial ear infection occurs when fluid gathers in the middle ear, behind the eardrum, and becomes infected with bacteria. This usually occurs in the context of a cold, usually several days after the cold begins, and frequently when parents believe the cold should be over. Frequently the baby's fever comes back, she becomes miserable—sometimes inconsolable—and feeding almost always decreases. The pressure from fluid behind the eardrum is usually the most troublesome symptom for the baby.

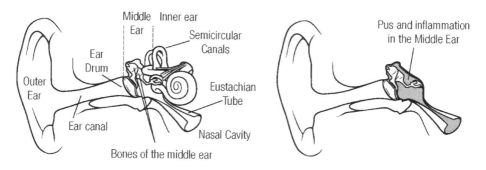

Babies have tiny passages in their ears that easily become infected. Most infections are viral, will pass with time, and will not benefit from antibiotics. Bacterial infections hurt because of the pus and pressure that build up in the middle ear and press on the eardrum, which can become inflamed.

Most ear infections are viral, which means that no bacteria are involved, so antibiotics do not help. The difference between viral and bacterial ear infections is that in viral infections the fluid that gathers behind the eardrum is not pus; it's clear fluid, but this does not make it less painful.

Getting a Trustworthy Diagnosis

The problem with diagnosing an acute bacterial ear infection is that babies are small, they wriggle a lot, and getting a good look at their eardrums is difficult to do without a fair amount of experience. If you bring your baby to a medical professional to look in her ears, make sure the person you're seeing has a lot of experience examining ears. As paradoxical as this sounds, the emergency department may not be the best place to go since emergency department doctors, especially those that specialize in adult medicine, may not have a lot of experience looking in infants' ears. They therefore tend to err on the side of treatment and might give prescriptions for antibiotics to parents of babies that don't actually have acute bacterial ear infections. If it is at all possible to wait until you can bring your baby to see an experienced pediatrician, she may be spared the risks of unnecessary treatment.

For the purposes of this book, which deals with babies less than six months old, the advice is different than for older babies and children. The American Academy of Pediatrics recommends that babies younger than six months old with acute bacterial ear infections should all be treated with antibiotics.

The key to treating an ear infection at any age is pain relief. No parent ever brought a baby to see me and said, "Doc, I'd like you to kill the *Streptococcus pneumoniae* that's growing in my daughter's middle ear space." Parents bring me babies who are miserable and who aren't eating. *That's* what parents want me to fix.

I often remind parents that no antibiotic ever made a baby eat better or sleep better and that antibiotics are not painkillers. The mainstay of the treatment for ear infections, then, is symptom control. For babies younger than six months, unfortunately the options are limited. The only comfort medication that is recommended for babies less than six months old is acetaminophen (Tylenol). Tylenol tends to be a less-than-ideal painkiller, but I cannot recommend the more effective ibuprofen (Motrin/Advil) because it tends to be too harsh on a little baby's stomach. Even if I give a baby antibiotics for her ear infection, it is essential that I treat the baby's pain with Tylenol. Any doctor who gives antibiotics for ear infections and doesn't talk about treating pain is not doing the baby any favors.

Teething

If the ear infection is the bogeyman of pediatrics, teething is vice-bogeyman. Historically, teething has been blamed for every malady of infancy, from fever, to diarrhea, to rashes... even to infant death.

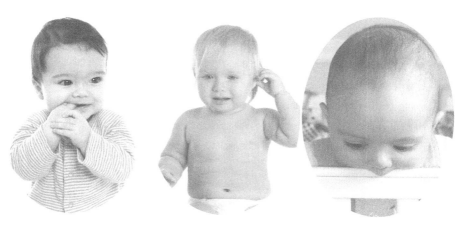

Babies often show signs of teething starting at four months. They drool, cry, fuss, sometimes pull their ears, and gum fingers and anything else they can get into their mouths. Until a baby is six months old and can take ibuprofen, there are no good remedies for the irritation of erupting teeth. The first tooth may appear at six or seven months.

Even though teething is not actually deadly, it can be incredibly bothersome to an infant. Teething behavior usually begins around four months of age with seemingly excessive drooling. Parents complain of having to change soaked bibs on their baby several times per day. A teething baby also tends to bite down on anything that she gets in her mouth—unfortunately, on occasion, mom's nipple. These symptoms do not mean teeth are about to erupt: In fact, symptoms of teething can precede the appearance of teeth by as long as eight months.

One of the classic signs of teething is ear pulling. No one knows for sure why teething babies pull on their ears. One theory is that pain from the gums is felt, or "referred," to the ears. Another theory states that the baby tries anything to make the pain go away, including ear pulling. The problem with ear pulling is that the parents may believe that their baby has an ear infection. Most of the fussy, ear-pulling babies I see in my office have perfectly normal ears and instead are teething. This so-called teething

The Deadly Teething Period

In the early part of the twentieth century, teething frequently appeared as a cause of death on birth certificates in Great Britain because even physicians believed teething was a dangerous and possibly deadly condition. It was believed that the pressure of nascent teeth was enough to cause inflammation that unleashed a cascade of events leading to death. Of course, the theory was eventually disproved, but not before an unhappy history of the treatment of teething was written.

Physicians (there were no pediatricians *per se* until the 1920s) seeing babies in their clinics were so concerned about the pressure caused by budding teeth that they often cut infant gums with scalpels to "release" the teeth and avoid harmful consequences. There are published case reports of some infants being submitted to this "treatment" more than once per day.

Another unfortunate teething remedy used until as recently as the mid-twentieth century is Calomel, a mercury-containing product that today is known to be a poison without any known therapeutic effects.

syndrome is so well described that it even has its own international classification of diseases (ICD) number!

There are myriad teething products on the market today, from homeopathic teething tablets (containing only calcium chloride, that is, chalk), to analgesic gels and a variety of biting toys. Parents freeze wet washcloths to give to their babies to gnaw. The characteristic that all these products share is that none of them work very well, if they work at all. The pain from budding teeth is an itch that no product or device seems to scratch. Even the gels that numb the skin of the gums do nothing for the deep discomfort that the baby feels.

A Tip from Dr Rob:

Simple Relief from Teething

I find that rubbing one's finger across a teething baby's gum line provides fast relief. The problem is that, as much as your baby may enjoy it, you cannot keep rubbing her gums all day long.

As with ear infections, I'm disappointed that the only truly effective teething medication, ibuprofen, is too harsh to give to babies less than six months old. Often Tylenol is the only medication I can offer, though it is not nearly as effective as I would like.

Reflux

Reflux is a lot more common than popularly believed. To be precise, I am referring to "gastroesophageal reflux," that is, milk that passes in the wrong direction: from stomach to esophagus rather than from stomach to intestines. Milk that starts in the stomach and ends up on the floor, by definition, is refluxed milk. All babies reflux to some extent. A small subset of babies, however, have bothersome symptoms associated with their reflux. These symptoms are pain and failure to gain weight. Lesser symptoms that parents bring to my attention are nasal congestion (caused by milk) and the mess and smell that regurgitated milk causes.

All reflux is by definition "acid reflux" since the contents of the stomach are acidic, so any milk that makes it to the stomach is acidified. That's why I avoid using the redundant expression "acid reflux." If the baby is not bothered by refluxing milk all day long, it does not mean that the refluxed liquid is not acidic, only that the baby's esophagus may be tougher than normal.

Reflux rises to the level of a medical problem only if it negatively affects the baby, either by causing her pain or by depriving her of enough calories to gain weight (because those calories are ending up on the floor). If a refluxing baby does not seem to be in pain and if she is gaining weight well, then there is nothing to fix. This kind of reflux is not a medical problem; it is a "janitorial" problem.

How can you tell if your baby's reflux is bothering her? The signs will not be subtle. Usually just after starting to eat and continuing for several minutes after she finishes, the baby fusses, squirms, and cries. She may gag and cough while feeding. If the acidity particularly bothers her, she may arch her back, grimace, and her face may turn colors from deep red to purple. These symptoms may not occur every time the baby eats, but true reflux occurs more than once and usually several times per week. If a baby is both bottle- and breast-fed, parents often report that the troubling symptoms occur more often after bottle-feeding than after breast-feeding. This is because there is more swallowed air in bottles that might rise in the form of bubbles and worsen reflux.

If your baby coughs and gags throughout feeding every time you feed her and does so from day one, you should tell your pediatrician right away. He may want to see you in the office to observe you and your baby. Some abnormalities of the baby's esophagus may be to blame and may require more investigation. This is rare and only occurs with babies that cough and gag from the day of birth every single time they feed.

Another sign that you should call the pediatrician is if the baby is not merely spitting up, but spitting across the room. Projectile vomiting may indicate a condition called *pyloric stenosis*, in which the muscle that closes off the outlet of the stomach becomes too muscular and stops opening properly. It is more common in boys and usually becomes evident at about two to six weeks of life. It's a condition that requires surgery to fix and the outcomes are good.

Finally, if the baby is spitting up not milk but green or yellow material, likely bile, this could indicate another surgical emergency such as a twisted, or "malrotated" intestine. Both pyloric stenosis and malrotation are rare. Garden-variety gastroesophageal reflux is extremely common.

Gravity maneuvers

If I determine that none of the worrisome signs are present and that the baby is gaining weight appropriately, my first therapeutic step is to employ what I call "gravity" maneuvers. Since reflux must fight gravity to get out of a baby's body, it makes sense to exploit gravity to the baby's advantage. Try keeping the baby's body angled up 30 degrees at all times except when changing her diaper. Place a wedge or other suitable object under the cushion on which the baby sleeps, but never place a pillow under your baby's head! Doing so may kink the baby's airway, making it difficult for her to breathe. Placing the baby in the car seat is sometimes effective, but for some particularly reflux-y babies the slightly curled "abdominal crunch" position of the car seat may actually worsen the reflux. If the car seat experiment fails, I encourage parents to use only the 30-degree wedge. After feeding, if at all possible, it helps if you can hold the baby upright for at least 15 to 20 minutes (for instance, in a baby carrier that permits an upright posture).

Meds for reflux

Sometimes gravity techniques aren't enough to keep the baby from feeling pain from reflux. In cases such as these, I usually prescribe ranitidine, commonly known as Zantac, an old and proven antacid that comes in a formulation for babies. Keep in mind, however, that ranitidine does not prevent reflux from happening; it only makes the reflux less painful.

There are currently no prescription or over-the-counter medications that are permissible to give to babies to prevent the mechanical phenomenon of reflux. If a baby is having more of a problem with gaining weight than with pain because of the huge amount of reflux she's having, my next step is to recommend giving thickened feeds by adding rice cereal to pumped breast milk or to formula.

Sometimes a baby's fussiness with feeds doesn't respond to our usual anti-reflux treatments. If this is the case, I often shift the focus to the contents of what the baby is eating. Specifically, I investigate whether the baby may be sensitive to something in breast milk or formula. If the baby is exclusively breast-fed, I often recommend an "elimination diet," meaning complete removal of certain items from mom's diet. The most likely suspect is cow's milk, so mom needs to remove *all* dairy products, including foods containing the milk proteins casein and whey, from her diet. If that doesn't work, I discuss with the mother other foods to eliminate. For formula-fed babies, switching to a soy-based formula may help. If this doesn't seem to be working, switching to a type of predigested elemental formula may (see Chapter 4 for more on formula options).

These anti-reflux approaches are best discussed with your pediatrician. Your pediatrician should weigh and examine your baby, and then you can discuss the best way to proceed. Much infantile reflux resolves by six months of age and virtually all of it resolves by twelve months. In the meantime, however, you and your pediatrician want to make those months as pleasant and pain-free as possible for your reflux-y baby.

Constipation

I have a brief and specific definition of constipation: **pain**. The frequency with which a baby poops is not at all important. The classic teaching is that a healthy, full-term, exclusively breast-fed baby may pass stool once per week and never suffer any cramps or colicky pain. At the other extreme, if a baby poops three times per day but strains and struggles for hours every day to produce those poops and finds relief only after pooping, then no one could argue with the suggestion that this baby is constipated. There is no ideal number of times per day that a baby should poop. The only goal is that she poops without pain.

The exception to my definition is a baby with an anal fissure, a small tear in the skin that can result from forceful passage of stool. Sometimes parents will see flecks of bright red blood in the stool. For an anal fissure, I recommend a spot of antibiotic cream three times per day. Fortunately, this part of a baby's anatomy heals quickly.

Constipation should also be differentiated from colic, which I discussed in Chapter 5. Finally, there are some food sensitivities or food allergies that may give a baby symptoms difficult to differentiate from the symptoms of constipation. These are the kinds of issues that you can work through with the aid of your pediatrician.

For most babies who need relief from passing painful poop, gentle methods work best to start. Since the goal is to make stool easier to pass, the simplest method is to add more water to the intestine. Since you should never give pure water to a baby less than six months old, I recommend sugar-water. The recipe is simple: one ounce of filtered water plus one level teaspoon of table sugar. You can give an ounce of sugar-water to a baby up to three times per day until you achieve the desired effect. Often one dose is sufficient.

If sugar-water is not soothing the baby's pain and helping her poop, then I recommend stepping up to diluted prune juice. I recommend buying pure prune juice, the kind you wouldn't drink for any other reason but *this* reason. Many parents in my practice boil their own prunes and give the baby the cooled-down runoff. As with sugar-water, I recommend one ounce of the diluted mixture, which ends up being one-half ounce water and one-half-ounce prune juice. Like sugar-water, you can give this mixture up to three times per day until you achieve success.

If neither sugar-water nor diluted prune juice is helping the baby with her pain, I usually go to a gentle, so-called osmotic laxative (like Miralax) that is sold over the counter in pharmacies. The benefit of Miralax is that it stays inside the intestine and is never absorbed by the baby's body. It simply helps pull more water into the colon to help make poop easier to pass.

Sometimes I get a call from a mother whose baby is so miserable from her constipation that she won't stop screaming in pain. In these cases I recommend giving a glycerin suppository such as those sold for infants in pharmacies. I never use suppositories as my first-line treatment for constipation because, unlike the other treatments listed above, suppositories tend to be habit-forming. That is to say, it is too easy for a baby to become dependent on the suppository in order to poop. I recommend using suppositories only when all else fails and only to help relieve a miserable baby.

Conjunctivitis

Conjunctivitis is simply a word that refers to inflammation of the invisible layer covering the eye and the inside of the eyelids, the *conjunctiva*. It is usually characterized by redness of the white part (called the *sclera*) of the eye and a copious discharge that is usually yellow or green. There are several causes of conjunctivitis, only one of which, bacterial conjunctivitis, requires treatment. The others are viral, allergic, and traumatic conjunctivitis (as when the baby gets poked in the eye). Allergic conjunctivitis is exceedingly rare in babies, so I'll omit it from this discussion. Two rare causes of conjunctivitis in small babies, herpes and chlamydia, are special cases that are beyond the scope of this chapter. Consult with your pediatrician if you have any doubts about what might be causing your baby's conjunctivitis.

The major difference between viral and bacterial conjunctivitis is the amount of goop that the infected eye produces. In viral conjunctivitis there is little discharge, whereas in bacterial conjunctivitis the yellow material fairly flows out of the eye, reaccumulating soon after being wiped away. If the infant's eyelashes stick together with the goop the eye produces, the conjunctivitis is probably bacterial.

A baby contracts bacterial conjunctivitis in the same way she gets viral conjunctivitis, most often by contact with a person who is ill. Good hand washing is the best way to prevent spread of both types of conjunctivitis.

One condition that imitates conjunctivitis deserves mention here: a narrow or blocked tear duct. The tear duct is located at the inside (nose-side) corner of each eye. The eye produces tears constantly and they drain through these ducts into the nose. In babies, tear ducts are tiny and clog easily. Small amounts of yellow or green goop may accumulate in the eye (less than would occur from the other causes of conjunctivitis), and the eye may tear up frequently. For narrow tear ducts, I recommend wiping the goop away with a warm washcloth and then giving a gentle massage with your pinky finger from just under the nose-side corner of the eye down and out toward the cheek. This is best done while the baby is eating, since if you touch a baby's face like this when she isn't eating, she will root around and look for a nipple that isn't there. Some mothers put a drop of breast milk in the eye for the same purpose. This is an ancient home remedy that seems to work, very likely because of natural enzymes in breast milk that break up the proteins gumming up the tear duct.

Upper respiratory viruses that cause viral conjunctivitis aren't treated with any standard medication. Viruses go away on their own and don't leave any signs that they were there. Bacterial conjunctivitis, on the other hand, should be treated, not only because it is highly contagious but also to reduce the pain and discomfort of the infection.

The dirty little secret of conjunctivitis

It turns out that you can treat most bacterial conjunctivitis with an over-the-counter antibiotic ointment, but most people do not know about this cure. I have been treating acute bacterial conjunctivitis this way in myself and in the children in my practice for

How I Discovered This "Dirty Little Secret"

Several years ago I received in the mail a package insert describing the contents of prescription-strength Neosporin ophthalmic ointment for the treatment of acute bacterial conjunctivitis. I read the ingredients list: Neomycin, Polymixin B, Bacitracin, hydrolatum... and nothing else. "That's it?" I asked myself, incredulously. These are precisely the ingredients of pharmacy-brand, triple antibiotic ointments. Then why is this one available by prescription and the others are sold over the counter? It turns out that the reason has to do only with the rules and regulations governing the factories where the various drugs are produced. The differences are so small as to make no difference in the purity and reliability of the two products.

Just to be sure, I consulted with a colleague of mine, an ophthalmologist, who at the time had been practicing for 40 years. "Is it true that prescription-strength antibiotic ointment is the same as the over-the-counter stuff?" I asked him. "Yes," he replied, "It's the same stuff." I have since run into colleagues who also use over-the-counter antibiotic ointments for acute bacterial conjunctivitis and, like me, they've kept their secret within the confines of their practices. And so have I, until now.

over ten years. The cure rate is high and the side effects are the same or fewer than those I've experienced with prescription medications. The fact that you can treat acute bacterial conjunctivitis without the help of a doctor is one of the dirty little secrets of pediatrics. I call it a dirty little secret because if it became widely known that this treatment was possible, it would eliminate many office and emergency department visits.

The over-the-counter medication I am suggesting comes in a tube that usually says, "Not for use in eye," only because the FDA has not approved the medication for this use. But the same goes for a great number of prescription medications that I prescribe as a pediatrician. If pediatricians prescribed only those medications that were approved by the FDA and that had been extensively tested in children, we'd have precious little medication at our disposal! I consider more than ten years of successful use in the children in my practice (and self-application) to be enough evidence for the safety and efficacy of this treatment.

The medications are the triple antibiotic combination found in the brand-name ointment Neosporin. They are Neomycin, Polymixin B, and Bacitracin. In Neosporin there are additives such as palm oil, so I don't like to recommend the name brand. There are also over-the-counter preparations that contain a painkiller. I do not recommend these either. You want to buy a pharmacy-brand ointment containing only these three antibiotics in a hydrolatum base.

First, wipe away as much goop as you can with a warm terrycloth washcloth. Then place a small dab of the antibiotic ointment on the tip of a clean pinky finger and place that dab in the corner of each eye. You don't need to peel down the eyelid or squeeze the ointment directly into the eye. If you place those dabs in the corners of the eye, as the baby blinks the medication spreads into the eye. Repeat three times a day for three or four days. It's best to treat both eyes, even if only one eye is goopy and red, because the opposite eye is likely going to get infected if it is not already infected.

In the event that the eye gets redder instead of clearer or if the infection appears to be getting worse and not better, contact your pediatrician. This could be because your baby is sensitive to one of the antibiotics in the ointment. I must stress that some babies will be sensitive to any antibiotic, and many babies in my practice have had adverse reactions to erythromycin, the prescription antibiotic usually prescribed for these babies.

Baby Medicines at Home

There are truly only a small number of medications that you ought to have at home in case you need them for your less-than-six-month-old baby. I have mentioned several of them throughout the course of this chapter. Infant acetaminophen (Tylenol) is the only "comfort medicine" and fever reducer that I recommend. As I mentioned before, ibuprofen (Motrin/Advil) is a bit too hard on the lining of a baby's stomach to recommend for this age group.

Every home should have at least one tube of antibiotic ointment, which is excellent for any cuts or breaks in the skin to prevent infection. Hydrocortisone 1% cream is excellent for eczema and other itchy skin conditions. For yeasty diaper rashes there is an over-the-counter preparation of the anti-fungal clotrimazole (Lotrimin). I recommend consulting with your pediatrician before using any of these products on a baby's skin.

For allergic reactions, the antihistamine diphenhydramine (Benadryl) is available in infant and children's preparations. I recommend always contacting a physician before giving diphenhydramine to a baby—first to get the correct dose; second, and most importantly, to check to see whether a more serious allergic reaction might be occurring.

Earlier in this book I mentioned various homeopathic products such as teething tablets. Unlike many of my colleagues, I have no deep-seated objection to the use of homeopathy. The major feature that homeopathic products have going for them is that they are safe, so they are extremely unlikely to do harm to your baby. I cannot vouch for their efficacy; in fact, I don't believe they work at all. But if you give them to your baby and they seem to do the trick, then by all means go ahead.

Keeping Your Baby Healthy while Traveling

To help prevent illnesses while you're traveling, see the section on "Taking the Show on the Road" in Chapter 3.

When Daycare Calls

Notice this section is not titled "*If* Daycare Calls." Sooner or later, your daycare provider is going to call you. In many states, credentialed providers are required to call parents for symptoms like fever, rashes, or loose poops. Often when the provider calls, he or she is doing so to ask you to come pick up your baby because she's sick.

In my experience, babies do not often begin to show symptoms of their illness at day-care: They are usually already sick at home. I realize that the pressures from employers are real and serious, but as a pediatrician I cannot recommend that you bring a child to daycare you if suspect she may be ill. In fairness, however, even in a perfect world where parents are diligent and miss work to stay home with their sick babies, illnesses would still find their way into daycare settings. This is because so many illnesses show no symptoms in the early stages.

If the daycare provider asks you to pick up your baby, you don't really have a choice. What you should *not* do is call the pediatrician before you've picked up your baby and seen her for yourself. Remember that you know this baby better than anybody on Earth. You are best equipped to decide if your baby is sick enough to require a doctor's attention. I recommend that you take your baby home and observe her for a short while before calling the doctor. More likely than not that you are in a better position to care for her than even the doctor is.

Many parents tell me that their child will not be permitted back at daycare until "cleared" by a physician. The truth is that your pediatrician does not live with you and cannot determine when 24 hours have elapsed since the child's last fever or whether that poop constitutes "diarrhea" or not. If the daycare provider truly needs physician input, I recommend that the provider speak to the doctor directly (only with the parents' written permission) and explain why the child needs an office visit. Your pediatrician works for you and your baby. She doesn't work for your daycare provider.

Calling the Doctor

If you have concerns of any kind about your baby's health, call your doctor. If it's an emergency, or you have a question as to whether it's an emergency, call any time. There are some general rules of thumb for knowing when to stay at home, when to call the doctor, when to go straight to the emergency department, and when to call 911.

Unless advised by your doctor, you should not take your child to the emergency department for the following reasons:

- Fever
- Ear pain/infection
- Flu

- Colds

- Minor sprains

- Nausea

- Stomach pain

- Headaches

- Sore throat

Call 911 if your child

- is not breathing or is turning blue;

- has sudden unconsciousness or cannot be awakened;

- is having a seizure (convulsing); or

- has severe unstoppable bleeding.

Go to the emergency department if your child has

- severe breathing difficulty;

- multiple or serious injuries, including fractures (broken bones); or

- a severe allergic reaction (swollen lips, swollen tongue, difficulty breathing).

The value of email

Many practices, mine included, afford parents the opportunity to email the doctor with questions that fall below the level of urgency of needing to speak to the pediatrician ASAP. I find that email is a successful system for the non-urgent physician inquiry and lends itself better to these inquiries than a phone call. This is especially true of *rashes*.

Rashes or anything that appears on skin are notoriously difficult to describe in words. Even though physicians have developed an extensive vocabulary to describe the shape, color, and character of things on the skin, *even we* have difficulty describing rashes over the phone. How much more difficult must it be for a parent!

This is the twenty-first century, and text messages are great, but they tend to arrive at inconvenient times, as opposed to emails, which can be answered when the doctor has time. If the issue is urgent, phone calls or text messages are perfectly appropriate—if it isn't an emergency, your doctor will appreciate an email!

How to Easily Document Skin and Other Conditions

Many parents are able to send me emails with high-resolution photographs—even videos—of skin and other conditions either from digital cameras or from their cell phones. These photographs make it much easier to diagnose a skin condition than a verbal description over the phone does. Making a treatment decision becomes easier as well.

That's why email is so valuable for communication with the doctor. More often than not these emails can spare tired parents the trouble of having to dress up their baby and haul her to the doctor!

How to make the most of "sick visits"

"Sick visits," also known as "unscheduled visits," are usually shorter than well visits, primarily because you will be discussing one specific problem with the doctor. The sequence of events that occurs during a sick visit has been more or less the same since the dawn of medicine. The doctor enters the room and says hello to everyone present. It's my practice to try and make a big show of saying hello to the baby. The baby is usually feeling bad and is scared to boot, so giving her a nice hello is essential. Then the doctor sits and listens to your story. It's best to give the story of the child's illness in chronological order, from the beginning of the first symptom to the present. As with phone calls, tell the doctor about all the symptoms that worry you and be sure to tell him or her about any "bad stories" you've heard about babies who had the same symptoms.

Then the doctor will wash hands and examine the baby. The exam will be a "focused" exam—focused on those parts of the baby that are most likely related to her symptoms. It may help the doctor to hold the baby during the exam. The baby is small and most of the exam is easy to do in a caregiver's arms. The baby will feel more comfortable and is less likely to be frightened and begin to cry. Some of the exam may have to be done on an exam table. We expect the baby may cry at this point!

When You Call the Doctor

A Tip from Dr Rob:

Before you call the office, these are the key pieces of information the doctor will want to know:

- *How old is your baby?* Different symptoms matter at different ages. The age of the baby is a critical piece of information for the doctor!

- *What are the worrisome symptoms (besides fever!)?* Does the baby smile (older than two months, of course)? Does the baby make eye contact? Is she at all playful? Can she drink? (This last question is very important.)

- *How long has your baby been sick?* If the baby became ill yesterday, the temptation is to say that the baby has been ill for "two days," though in fact the baby has been sick for fewer than 24 hours. It's important to tell the doctor *on what day* the baby became ill.

- *What are your specific concerns?* For instance, ask questions like, "Will my baby get dehydrated?" If there are specific illnesses you are afraid of, say so! The doctor can't read your mind: If your aunt told you that her friend's baby had the same symptoms as your baby and that baby ended up being very sick, you should communicate this story to your doctor!

- *What remedies/medicines have you already tried?*

Finally, the doctor will give an opinion about what's going on with the baby, and together parents and doctor will decide how to proceed. Most often the next step will be a discussion of over-the-counter "comfort" medicines. Occasionally the doctor will write a prescription. Rarely the baby may need further testing to determine the source of the problem.

Hopefully the doctor will make sure that all your questions have been answered. If not, please ask the questions again! The visit should not end until you are satisfied that you have a plan of action. It's always a good idea to verify with the doctor that you should contact the office again if the baby does not get better when the doctor predicts she will.

Notes:

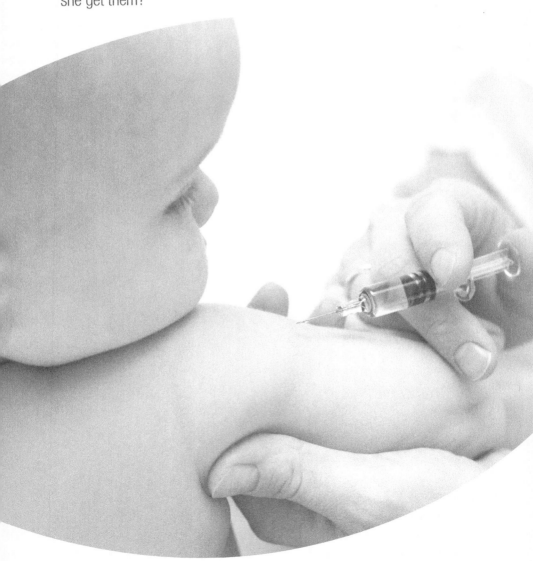

Chapter Highlights

- What is the history of vaccines, and what are all those vaccine controversies about?
- What did we learn from the vaccine wars?
- Is it safe to delay giving vaccines?
- Which vaccines are safe and effective for my baby, and when should she get them?

Chapter 9

Vaccinations

Parents are understandably anxious about vaccines. There is an enormous amount of rumor and Internet chatter about vaccines. Many parents believe that vaccine safety is a subject of great controversy today. The truth is that there is *no controversy*, despite what you may have read. The effects of vaccines have been studied numerous times using very large populations (sometimes entire countries). No study has been able to find *any* negative health consequences of vaccines. To the contrary: The development of vaccines is one of the greatest achievements in human history!

The history of vaccines has not been without bumps in the road, however, and these unfortunate bumps—all in the distant past—continue to fuel the fires of anti-vaccine activists. The story of those triumphs and how your baby will benefit from them is the subject of this chapter.

Vaccines and Their Discontents

Next to the invention of indoor plumbing and synthetic fibers for clothing, the development and introduction of vaccines represents one of the greatest public health triumphs of the modern era. It is hardly an exaggeration to state that vaccines have saved millions of lives that otherwise would have been lost to the previously devastating diseases of childhood.

Unlike any other public health advance in the history of humankind, however, vaccines are unique in that their history has been riddled with controversy, not to mention popular discontent with the procedure, since the early eighteenth century. Since then, major public controversies have broken out over the polio vaccine, the diphtheria-tetanus-pertussis (DTP) vaccine, and the measles-mumps-rubella (MMR) vaccine. Although you may be more familiar with this last vaccine controversy, you might not be aware of the earlier controversies and the lessons from those debates that might inform our attitude toward modern vaccines.

History

The word "vaccine" derives from the Latin word for the cowpox virus, *Variola vaccinia*. The history of the very first vaccinations gives us a great deal of insight into the benefits—and the controversies—surrounding vaccination, some of which continue to this day.

Smallpox and the variolation procedure

The story of vaccines is forever linked to the first disease ever eradicated by human agency: smallpox (*Variola major* or *Variola minor*). Smallpox was a highly contagious viral disease that probably began infecting humans about 10,000 years ago. The virus attacked skin and mucus membranes, causing disfiguring blisters that left deep scars, or pockmarks, on the skin of survivors. Approximately 30% to 35% of victims of smallpox died of the disease; the fatality rate in children was even higher, about 80%.

Smallpox prevention efforts are known to have begun in China during the Ming Dynasty (sixteenth century), although there is reason to believe the practice is much older. The method consisted of either asking the uninfected individual to inhale dried pustules from the victim of smallpox or scratching material from the pustule into the skin of the healthy person. Lasting immunity from smallpox resulted from the procedure. Unfortunately, there was as much as a 2% chance of dying of smallpox from this procedure, and those who were treated could still pass the illness to others.

This immunization process, known as variolation, came to the West in the early eighteenth century as visitors to China brought back eyewitness accounts, and word spread via medical journals. Cotton Mather, a prominent Puritan minister in Boston, Massachusetts, read one of these journals. In 1721, the Massachusetts Bay Colony was in the midst of a smallpox outbreak that eventually killed 844 people, most of them children. Mather implored local lay physician Zabdiel Boylston to begin a variolation campaign.

Boylston variolated 242 individuals at risk for contracting smallpox. Six of them died of smallpox as a result of the procedure. The public outcry was enormous. Objections from physicians as well as laypeople ranged from outrage against efforts that, in the minds of some citizens, seemed to "contravene the will of God" to criticism of the seemingly foreign medical procedure (preventive medicine of any kind was unknown in eighteenth-century America). An angry citizen threw a turpentine grenade into Mather's home. Boylston was arrested and released only after promising never to perform the procedure again. Nevertheless, many Bostonians sought out Boylston in secret, hoping to protect themselves and their children from smallpox.

Jenner introduces inoculation

Meanwhile in Great Britain, unbeknownst to Mather and Boylston, physician Edward Jenner (1749–1823) was developing a safer, effective way of preventing smallpox.

Jenner noticed that English milkmaids never had pockmarked faces. He postulated that these milkmaids were immune to smallpox by virtue of their having already contracted the nonfatal bovine version of the illness, cowpox (*Variola vaccinia*). Jenner experimented by inoculating an eight-year-old boy with material derived from pustules on the fingers of a milkmaid. (This was well before the era of Institutional Review Boards and informed consent. Suffice it to say that such an experiment would never happen today!) The boy developed some uneasiness and fever but did not become ill. Later, Jenner inoculated the boy with smallpox pustules. The boy did not become ill. Jenner repeated the procedure numerous times, all with similar results. Inoculation with cowpox worked because of similarities between the smallpox and cowpox vaccines. Jenner obviously could not have known about antibodies and immune responses, but his careful observations and effective (if crude) scientific techniques saved millions of lives. The era of vaccination had begun.

Despite these successes, there was considerable public backlash. People objected to having a cow virus forcibly introduced into their bodies. A fashionable rumor arose that a vaccinated person would begin sprouting bovine appendages.

Vaccinia and the eradication of smallpox

Cowpox vaccine was eventually replaced by a related, less-controversial vaccine. This vaccine, though thousands of times safer than Jenner's cowpox vaccine, nevertheless carried risks along with benefits. About 1 in 1,000 people vaccinated for the first time developed serious but nonfatal reactions to the vaccine and 1 per million died as a result.

A worldwide campaign to eradicate smallpox began in the 1950s. The campaign was so successful that vaccination in the United States was halted in 1972. The last reported naturally occurring case of smallpox was reported in Ethiopia in 1977. Thereafter, smallpox was declared eradicated, making it the first human disease to disappear by virtue of human agency.

Polio

The next major human disease on track for elimination is poliomyelitis, or polio. Until development of the polio vaccine in the mid-twentieth century, polio was the leading cause of paralysis in previously healthy children. Polio was particularly scary because it often began as a simple "stomach bug" but progressed over a few days to include a stiff neck and a frightening loss of muscle strength. The grandparents of children currently in my practice remember polio scares in which public swimming pools were closed and families canceled trips to ponds and lakes where polio was rumored to be spreading. There are still people alive today who themselves contracted polio as children or who know someone who did. Entire wards of hospitals used to be filled with large cylindrical breathing machines known as "iron lungs," designed for children too weak to breathe on account of their polio-related paralysis. Some children lived the remainder of their shortened lives in iron lungs.

When I was a resident at Boston Children's Hospital in the 1990s, a bunch of us sneaked into the basement of the old building and found some of the iron lungs used to treat children with polio. Today, these machines stand as living testaments to an era that has almost ended.

A global eradication program was initiated in 1987, and it is anticipated to reach its successful conclusion in the early twenty-first century. When polio is eradicated, it will represent a public health victory even more impressive than the eradication of smallpox. Whereas smallpox is passed only from person to person, the virus causing polio can live for brief periods in water, making it much more difficult to wipe out with a vaccination campaign. Nevertheless, thanks to careful monitoring and extremely hard work on the part of thousands of public health workers, wild-type polio remains endemic in only three countries: Afghanistan, Pakistan, and Nigeria.

It is worth mentioning that the history of polio vaccination is not without its own controversies and challenges. In 1955, shortly after the release of a vaccine manufactured by Cutter Laboratories of Berkeley, California, hundreds of children began developing polio, apparently contracted from the vaccine. Many of these children became paralyzed as a result and several died.

It turned out that several batches of vaccine contained live virus that had not been properly inactivated by the manufacturing process. These were the days before batches of vaccines were tested for quality and purity before release to the public. As a result of this catastrophe, industry and governmental standards were tightened, as were purification and testing practices for all vaccines, but public confidence in the polio vaccine was shaken.

The dramatic decline in the number of cases of polio, however, was enough to convince a skeptical public of the value of the vaccine. Swimming pools reopened in the summer of 1956, and rumors of a child with a fever and stiff neck no longer sent waves of panic through a neighborhood. Polio was on the way to disappearing in the United States. Nevertheless, controversy dogged the polio vaccine into the 1990s, when a British journalist suggested that HIV had been introduced into human vaccines via oral polio vaccine. These claims were subsequently scientifically disproven.

The Americas were declared free of polio in 1994. It is unclear how long the United States will continue to recommend polio vaccination. I suspect that the large amount of travel between the three remaining endemic countries and the United States is the reason for our continued vigilance.

Diptheria-tetanus-pertussis

All three of these diseases caused disability and death in large numbers of children prior to the introduction of the separate vaccine campaigns against them. Since the 1970s, the most common type of vaccine directed against these diseases has come in combination, the DTP vaccine.

Diphtheria is caused by the bacterium *Corynebacterium diphtheriae*, which releases a toxin that causes a swelling of the throat that may close it completely. In the early twentieth century, pediatric training included instruction in how to perform a tracheostomy to provide an opening in the neck of a child severely affected by diphtheria. Since the development of an effective vaccine, the disease has been all but eradicated in the developed world.

Tetanus is caused by a bacterium found in the soil, *Clostridium tetani*, which also releases a toxin that causes painful muscle spasms throughout the body, often leading to the inability to breathe and death by suffocation. It is the effect on muscles of the face that gave tetanus its older name, lockjaw. In the developing world where the vaccine is not available, tetanus kills approximately 50,000 newborns every year. Today in the United States, there are 50 to 100 cases of tetanus per year, virtually all in unimmunized or incompletely immunized people.

Pertussis, or whooping cough, is caused by a bacterium called *Bordatella pertussis*. Infection with this bug causes symptoms that start out like those of a cold but rapidly progress into a vicious cough that often causes the sufferer to lose his breath and forces him to take a large, violent inhalation, or whoop. Even after the bacterial infection is gone, the cough can last for three months or more. Whereas pertussis is a huge annoyance for older children or adults, for babies it can be deadly.

Pertussis has become a substantial public health problem again after several years of increasing rarity in the United States and the rest of the developing world. Pertussis is the only vaccine-preventable infectious disease in the United States that is becoming more deadly, not less deadly. There are several reasons for this increase, but the major one is declining immunization rates. In large part, the drop in rates has been attributed to controversies surrounding the vaccine.

During the 1970s, an international controversy erupted following a report from Great Britain that several babies developed neurological impairments after taking the vaccine. Vaccination rates began to drop, with a subsequent rise in cases of whooping cough. A 1982 television documentary, *DPT: Vaccination Roulette*, as well as a 1991 book titled *A Shot in the Dark*, trumpeted the risk of the vaccine but minimized the benefits. Any connection between DTP vaccine and neurological damage was quickly disproved with careful epidemiologic study, but the damage was done. Several vaccine manufacturers decided that it was no longer worth their while to manufacture the vaccine after enduring long, expensive lawsuits and low profit margins. The rates of whooping cough began to rise as a result of both lowered rates of vaccination and vaccine shortages.

Another reason for the recent resurgence of pertussis in the United States is that the vaccine we currently have simply isn't very good. It only protects for five to ten years, and some believe it protects for an even shorter period. In the community where I work, there were so many outbreaks of pertussis in the middle schools that the state of Massachusetts began to mandate booster shots for children entering the seventh grade. The current Centers for Disease Control and Prevention (CDC) recommendation is that all adults be boosted against pertussis every ten years, but currently there is little or no public health effort in place to boost adults. The relatively poor efficacy of the vaccine, the lack of immunity in much of the adult population, and dropping vaccination rates are giving rise to our current spike in cases of pertussis. Diphtheria and tetanus, fortunately, have not reappeared in the United States, probably because their vaccines provide substantially better immunity against these bacteria than the pertussis vaccine does against pertussis.

Measles-mumps-rubella

Measles is a highly contagious viral infection that produces fever and cold symptoms followed by a characteristic rash all over the body. Measles continues to be a major cause of vaccine-preventable deaths worldwide, mostly in the developing world. Since measles is no longer endemic to the United States, the few cases that occur here every year are imported from other countries by unimmunized individuals.

Mumps is a relatively benign viral infection that causes uncomfortable swelling of the glands in the cheeks (the parotid glands), and in older boys and men can cause inflammation of the testicles (orchitis) that can lead to infertility.

Rubella, or German measles, is a relatively brief and mild illness characterized by fever and rash. Although rubella is benign for children, it is positively devastating for developing fetuses. If a mother contracts rubella prior to 20 weeks gestation, her baby may develop several severe birth defects, a constellation of symptoms called the congenital rubella syndrome. It was to prevent this syndrome that the rubella vaccine was developed.

At the time of this writing, in 2012, there is only one formulation of a vaccine against these three diseases, the measles-mumps-rubella, or MMR, vaccine. The controversy surrounding the MMR vaccine began in 1998 when a paper in the prestigious British journal, *The Lancet,* purported to demonstrate an association between the MMR vaccine and the development of autism. As a result, a firestorm erupted in Great Britain and the United States, and thousands of worried parents stopped vaccinating their children with MMR. As a result, there were outbreaks of measles in the UK.

Other researchers could not reproduce the findings in *The Lancet* paper. Considerable doubts about the scientific integrity of the paper and its lead author, Andrew Wakefield, led to the almost unprecedented retraction of the MMR-autism paper in 2010. Dr. Wakefield was subsequently found to have produced fraudulent research and was stripped of his license to practice medicine in the UK, but the damage was done. Among other things, Wakefield had already suggested in public that the various components of the MMR vaccine should be separated. This suggestion has led to the widespread misconception on the part of parents that vaccines should not be given together. There is no credible scientific evidence that it is harmful to give vaccines bundled together. Unfortunately, even though Dr. Wakefield's work has been discredited, the myths he promulgated have gained a life of their own.

Before Wakefield, measles was on the way to being eradicated, much like smallpox before it (and hopefully soon polio). But the Wakefield debacle has set back the campaign against measles by several years.

Thimerosal

As the furor over Wakefield's work was beginning to crest and decline, another vaccine controversy erupted, this time over the mercury-containing preservative Thimerosal. In 1997, the Food and Drug Administration (FDA) mandated a review of all food and pharmaceutical products containing mercury. Even though the review revealed no evidence that Thimerosal produced mercury poisoning or that mercury in vaccines caused any adverse effects, the U.S. Public Health Service and the American Academy of Pediatrics recommended that Thimerosal be removed from vaccines.

The anti-vaccination community that, as I have shown, had been active since 1721 leapt on the recommendation to remove Thimerosal as evidence that the substance was harmful. A paper in the non-peer-reviewed journal *Medical Hypotheses* in 2001 suggested a link between Thimerosal and autism.

Subsequently, numerous large epidemiological studies found no link whatsoever between Thimerosal and autism (or any adverse neurodevelopmental outcome), but once again the controversy shook public confidence. Even though at this point virtually all vaccines have had Thimerosal removed, public concern over *all* types of vaccine preservatives, including trace metals such as aluminum, have further depressed vaccination rates.

Lessons learned from the vaccine wars

Several common themes emerge from all the vaccine-related controversies that have emerged since the introduction of variolation in the eighteenth century.

First, **concerns over safety.** No vaccine is 100% safe. This remains true even today, though vaccines are immeasurably safer than the days when raw infected material was scratched into a healthy person's arm, and even since the 1950s Cutter Laboratories fiasco. The public demands and deserves a modicum of safety, always balanced against the risks of the disease targeted by the vaccine. Despite knowledge that variolation could be deadly, Massachusetts Bay Colony residents were willing to take the risk against the greater danger of contracting smallpox. Despite the well-publicized Cutter incident, Americans feared polio more than they feared the vaccine.

Second, **concerns over personal integrity.** Anglo-Saxons in particular have always been suspicious of authority. This is especially so when powerful authorities compel United States and British citizens to be injected with foreign substances, some of which may be toxic. Even though today the safety of vaccines is very high, the intrusion on the body represented by the injection of a needle triggers an instinctive repulsion in many people, especially in populations with long traditions of self-governance such as the United States and Great Britain. It should come as no surprise, then, that vaccine controversies emerge and thrive primarily in these two countries.

Finally, **concerns about efficacy.** In general, we accept a certain amount of risk as long as we can be reasonably sure of a benefit. When it comes to our health (and more so, the health of our children), we don't like to gamble. If we are going to absorb the risks of giving vaccines, even if those risks are small (pain at the site, fever, fussiness), we would like to know that our babies are going to become immune against a deadly disease. Historically, we have responded very positively to successful vaccination campaigns. There have been plenty of Nobel Prizes awarded to reflect our gratitude for vaccines.

These are the origins of our current attitudes toward vaccination. For parents making decisions about whether and when to vaccinate their baby, it's useful to know the rationale that underlies vaccination campaigns in general and how our contemporary vaccine schedule conforms (and deviates) from that framework.

When Do We Vaccinate, and Why?

The central unifying principle behind vaccination programs is *risk*. A community institutes a vaccine campaign when there is risk and suspends the campaign when the risk goes away. This is perhaps an oversimplification, but the principle holds throughout our history. An equally important consideration is severity of the risk. If the disease is fatal or crippling, the risk is obviously greater. Conversely, everyone is at risk for contracting the common cold, but the severity of the illness has never justified a full-scale campaign to develop a vaccine against cold viruses.

Smallpox in the eighteenth century is an example of severe risk. In 1721, in the midst of the first smallpox outbreak in 20 years, Cotton Mather and Zabdiel Boylston undertook a bold and dangerous variolation campaign. As another example, today when sporadic cases of measles or rubella appear, public health authorities spring into action and quickly immunize all possible contacts. I was one such possible contact when I was in college. University health officials learned that there had been a case of rubella in the dormitory where I lived. All of us dutifully lined up to receive an MMR booster, whether or not we were already immune, since the risk of a rubella outbreak (at least for the women of childbearing age in our community) was great enough in their opinion to justify a local immunization campaign.

Personal and public health

There are always at least two reasons to carry out a vaccination campaign: protection of individual health and protection of the public health. Clearly, you don't want your children to become seriously ill, particularly if the illness is vaccine-preventable. For communicable diseases, communities decide that they don't want sick people to spread their illnesses, placing others at risk of crippling complications or death.

All vaccines have the potential to protect your child against a disease if the vaccine "takes," meaning that the child develops immunity to the vaccine. As I mentioned earlier, not all children develop protective immunity to vaccines. On occasion your child may develop partial immunity to a virus or bacterium, enough to protect her from getting very sick. We've seen this phenomenon with the chicken pox vaccine, where some immunized children develop very mild cases of chicken pox. In these cases, however, the immunized children can still pass the virus to other non-vaccinated children.

Public health is more than just individual health multiplied over an entire population in a community. Public health officials, as agents of governments, are charged with keeping communities from getting sick because sick people cannot work or pay taxes. In communities with varieties of universal health care, sick people are expensive to take care of. Some experts refer to vaccination campaigns as "social contracts," in which individuals allow themselves to be injected with foreign substances, even if they object to the practice, for the sake of the community as a whole. Others say that the right of the individual to decide what does and doesn't enter his or her child's body trumps the government's interest in protecting public health.

But some vaccine campaigns are more than social contracts. Some have the backing of legal precedent. The landmark case from Massachusetts involved a man who refused to submit to a smallpox inoculation. He claimed that submission to the vaccine violated his liberty under the constitution. The Supreme Court of the United States decided otherwise (*Jacobson v. Commonwealth of Massachusetts*, 1905). The court ruled that the states can compel vaccination if there is grave risk to the public health.

The problem with *Jacobson* is that in the twenty-first century we are no longer faced with existential threats such as smallpox, and polio is close to worldwide eradication. Now that the public no longer faces such severe threats, the personal health justification for vaccination campaigns is much stronger than the public health justification. The challenge for public health officials in the twenty-first century is to make the case to the public that vaccination is in the best interests of their children and the public as a whole.

The Vaccines

For each vaccine, I describe the disease against which it protects (unless previously discussed) and give my recommendations about vaccination. See Appendix B for the full vaccine schedule.

Hepatitis B

Hepatitis is a liver infection that causes yellow skin and gastrointestinal symptoms. In its quiet, chronic form it can cause liver cancer, which is why the vaccine against hepatitis B has been touted as being the first anticancer vaccine in history. The vaccine is not effective against other types of hepatitis, such as types A and C.

Hepatitis B virus is acquired, for all intents and purposes, in only three ways: by being born to a mother with active hepatitis B; by having sex with someone with active hepatitis B; or by having one's skin punctured by a sharp object (accidentally or on purpose) that has been contaminated with the blood of someone who has active hepatitis B.

That's it. You may have noticed that with the exception of the first method (acquisition from your mother), infants are simply not at risk for contracting hepatitis B. Most mothers who now deliver in the United States have been tested for hepatitis B so that proper precautions can be taken to limit the chances that the baby might contract the disease.

While the hepatitis B vaccine appears to be safe and effective, the vaccine fails to meet the standard of vaccinating where there is risk. You may therefore ask why we give this vaccine to newborns before they leave the hospital. The answer is because we *can*. Hepatitis B vaccine has proven effective even when the first of the series of three shots is given on the first day of life. So although I support giving all the vaccines to all infants I believe the parents stand on very solid medical and ethical ground by delaying the hepatitis B vaccine.

Hemophilus Influenzae type B (Hib)

Hib is a bacterium that passes from person to person by direct contact or by droplets (coughs and sneezes). It should not be confused with the virus that causes influenza; they are totally different microbes! In the pre-vaccine era, Hib meningitis was a substantial cause of illness and death in the United States and Canada. Since the introduction of the vaccine in 1987, the incidence of Hib meningitis has dropped to almost zero.

Hib also causes a particularly nasty and deadly complication called epiglottitis. Epiglottitis is a sudden swelling of the cap on top of the windpipe (trachea) that closes whenever we swallow. When infected by Hib, the epiglottis swells and blocks the trachea. The victims, usually children, used to suffocate unless rescued by an emergency tracheostomy (making an artificial hole in the neck).

Many colleagues of mine who have been board-certified in pediatric emergency medicine for 20 years have never seen epiglottitis. On the other hand, I know colleagues who have practiced since the pre-Hib vaccine era. They remember children dying of Hib meningitis. They describe cases of children who came to their offices in the morning with ear infections and, despite starting antibiotics, died of Hib meningitis later that evening. These catastrophes, epiglottitis and Hib meningitis, have largely disappeared thanks to the vaccine.

Hib is one of the two vaccines that I strongly encourage parents who are thinking of delaying vaccines to reconsider. The recommended series is given at two, four, and six months, with a booster in the second year of life.

Pneumococcus

Streptococcus pneumoniae, also known as pneumococcus, is not to be confused with the bacterium that causes strep throat (that is *Streptococcus pyogenes*, a different bug). Pneumococcus is a common cause of serious bacterial infections in children, including pneumonia and meningitis. Like Hib, pneumococcus is also spread from person to person, either by direct contact or by droplets.

Since the introduction of the vaccine in 2002, the incidence of serious bacterial infections has declined dramatically.

Until recently, the vaccine routinely given to infants was directed against the seven most common types of pneumococcus. Now there is a vaccine directed against a total of 13 common types. Whereas the results of the pneumococcal vaccine campaign in the United States have not been as dramatic as those of the Hib vaccine, the declines in deaths and disease are nevertheless substantial. To parents contemplating delaying vaccines, this vaccine, like Hib, is one that I recommend giving according to the usual schedule at two, four, and six months, with a booster usually at the first birthday.

Diphtheria, tetanus, and acellular pertussis (DTaP)

The reason these three diseases are discussed together here is that for infants and young children, the triple vaccine is the only variety available. Though several companies manufacture DTaP, the various components are no longer manufactured separately for individual sale. I discussed all three diseases briefly earlier in the chapter.

The reason to discuss DTaP here is because one of the components, the P for pertussis (whooping cough), is a major cause of concern in the infant population. Diptheria and tetanus are terrible diseases, but they currently do not command the same amount of time, attention, and health care dollars that pertussis does. A significant *problem* with the DTaP vaccine is that the pertussis portion is not all that effective—immunity wanes over a decade. We've discovered that in order to reduce whooping cough in young babies, we need to revaccinate older children and adults, who are the major sources of whooping cough contagion for babies.

This problem is compounded in communities that have relatively high rates of vaccine-refusing parents. It turns out that vaccination rates do not need to drop substantially for the so-called herd immunity effect to disappear and place vulnerable individuals at risk. Herd immunity describes the number of members of a community (or herd, as the case may be) that one needs to vaccinate in order to reduce the number of susceptible individuals so much that the microbe in question has no one to infect. As a result, the non-vaccinated individuals are protected as well. The herd immunity threshold for pertussis is very high, estimated at 92% to 94%, meaning that at least 92% of the population must be vaccinated for non-vaccinated individuals to be protected as well. By comparison, the threshold for mumps is only 75%.

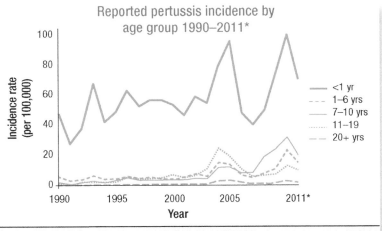

*2011 data are not yet finalized and subject to change. 2011 data were accessed July 5, 2012. *Source:* CDC, National Notifiable Diseases Surveillance System and Supplemental Pertussis Surveillance System

The pertussis vaccine (the P in DTaP) is not highly effective and needs to be readministered at ten-year intervals to confer immunity. As a result of its lower effectiveness and high herd immunity threshold, cases of whooping cough have been on the rise in the U.S. since about 1990. This chart illustrates that rise by age class: Infants under three months old are uniformly at greatest risk, followed by school-aged children aged seven to nineteen years (when immunity tends to wear off). Source: Centers for Disease Control.

Until we develop a better vaccine, greater than 95% of babies will need the DTaP vaccine in order to keep the unvaccinated babies (less than two months of age) out of harm's way. For this reason, I recommend giving DTaP to your baby at two, four, and six months of age, particularly if your baby will be attending daycare or any other environment where she may encounter an individual whose own immunity has waned and who has picked up whooping cough.

Polio

Since the late 1990s, polio vaccine is given only via injection. The live-attenuated drops vaccine is no longer given, primarily because it was so successful. The risk of contracting polio in the United States became so low that the risk of developing vaccine-related polio exceeded the risk of catching wild-type (normal) polio. When that happened, it no longer made sense to give U.S. children the live vaccine.

With a extremely low risk of contracting polio in the United States, many parents choose to delay the polio vaccine. According to the vaccinate-where-there-is-risk strategy, this makes sense. If, however, the family will be traveling to an area where polio is endemic, such as Pakistan, Afghanistan, or Nigeria, then polio vaccination is strongly recommended.

Rotavirus

Rotavirus causes a severe, sometimes serious, viral infection of the intestines that causes vomiting, diarrhea, and dehydration. Only in rare instances does the virus cause such severe diarrhea that death from dehydration occurs. Rotavirus is passed from person to person by contact with infected poop, so caregivers need to wash their hands carefully when changing diapers. Rotavirus is by no means the only virus that causes the stomach bug, but it is the only one for which we currently have a vaccine.

The stomach bug caused by rotavirus is common. In the pre-vaccine era, virtually every child on Earth contracted rotavirus by age five. In the United States, rotavirus used to cause 2.7 million cases of severe gastroenteritis in children every year, resulting in 60,000 hospitalizations and around 37 deaths.

An oral, live-attenuated vaccine against rotavirus—the newest infant vaccine in the United States—has been available for a few years. A previous version of the vaccine was pulled off the market because of fears that the vaccine might cause a rare form of intestinal obstruction, but this turned out not to be the case. The new vaccine has no such reported problems. After the vaccine was introduced, the effects were fairly dramatic and substantial. Although firm numbers are not yet available, preliminary reports indicate a substantial decline in hospitalizations and deaths from rotavirus.

The real reason for the introduction of the vaccine was not so much to reduce deaths, although that is a laudable goal. Any public health effort must calculate how many precious resources can be devoted to save lives. As cold-hearted as this seems, it is an essential calculation for us to make. The truth is that rotavirus is not a very deadly virus. It *does*, however, cause a substantial amount of human misery in the form of ill children, hospitalizations, and lost productivity at work. For these reasons, the cost-benefit analysis favors carrying out a vaccination campaign.

Many parents, considering the various points just made, decide to withhold the rotavirus vaccine. My view is that the risks of serious complications are low enough to justify the decision to give the vaccine.

Measles-mumps-rubella (MMR) and varicella

These vaccines are both given to children one year of age and older, and therefore fall out of the scope of this book. Nevertheless, both vaccines deserve some brief comment since the considerations regarding the decision to give or withhold these vaccines are the same as for the other vaccines discussed in this chapter.

In the section on vaccine controversies, I discussed measles, mumps, and rubella in more detail. I regard the MMR vaccine as both safe and effective. The question then becomes: Is it safe for parents to delay MMR? Many parents continue to be plagued by fears that the MMR vaccine causes autism and therefore decide to delay the vaccine until there is no question that the child does not have autism (usually by age two or older). Given the relatively low incidence of measles in our community, I regard the decision to delay MMR to be rational and safe.

If the decision is to forgo the MMR vaccine forever, however, I disagree. We have been lucky in recent years that measles outbreaks have been few in number and mild in severity. My concern is that if a substantial number of families decide to withhold MMR in a given community, then larger and more severe outbreaks might occur.

The varicella (chicken pox) vaccine is another story entirely. Chicken pox always has been an annoying, troublesome, but ultimately benign and self-limited disease of childhood. Its complications, though measurable, are rare, including death. The vaccine can prevent shingles later in life as well.

As with the rotavirus vaccine, the cost-benefit analysis to justify a vaccination campaign against chicken pox has to do with lost productivity at work, not with the complications of the illness. It turns out that at least one parent needs to stay at home with a child with chicken pox.

One Final Word about Vaccines

My guess is that if there had never been any controversy about vaccines, parents would probably line up out the door to get their children vaccinated against any disease. Even though this country enjoys a long and proud history of rugged individualism and suspicion of government, Americans have always generally been favorably disposed toward public health campaigns. Witness, for example, the long and strong history of environmentalism in the United States. Americans have supported large-scale environmental legislation such as the Clean Air Act and the Federal Water Pollution Control Act and have reaped benefits in the form of healthier air and safe drinking water.

Were it not for a few events in history, the foregoing discussion might have been unnecessary.

- What have you learned about your baby?
- What does the six-month milestone mean for how you view and treat your baby when she's sick?
- What other major milestones can you expect at six months?
- What are the consequences of viewing your baby as essentially a healthy being?

Chapter 10

Six Months and Beyond

Congratulations! You've reached the half-year mark. By this point, as I've described in this book, you've learned a lot about your own baby and even a fair amount about pediatrics.

Hey! I Know You!

Unlike the first several weeks of life described in Chapters 1 and 2, by six months you likely have a much better sense of what your baby is like. She has a personality by now, and she definitely has developed a personal relationship with each of her caregivers and possibly with siblings and extended family as well.

By now, though you may not realize it, you've become an experienced parent. You are a parent who knows what a normal baby looks and acts like, and you've become the undisputed expert at caring for at least one baby: yours. At this point no one on Earth knows this baby better than you do. You can trust your instincts about your baby: 99.99% of the time your instinct will be correct.

Hopefully by this time you've internalized the knowledge that you and you alone are the parent of this baby—not your parents, but *you!* Your judgments and decisions are the final ones because you own the responsibility for caring for your baby.

In return, you reap the rewards of getting to spend every day with a unique human being, a human being who will surprise you and make you smile almost every day. You are the most important person in the world to this child, and she will show you just how important you are to her by cleaving as close to you as a human being is able.

What's for lunch?

You've become an expert at feeding your baby, reading her hunger cues, and responding to them appropriately. In fact, your ability to read hunger cues has become so automatic you might not be aware that it is happening. You're ready to embark on the wonderful, messy journey that is feeding solids (see below).

Zzzzzzzz.......

By now your baby is sleeping through the night or almost through the night. Some parents complain to me that their six-month-old only sleeps six hours at night. I remind these parents that throughout most of the world six hours *is* through the night! If the baby is still waking to feed, there's good news: This phase of her life is about to end.

Easy, Baby!

You've become an expert in calming your baby, especially when she is crying. Reaching this milestone may have taken a fair amount of your own tears as well as hours of your sleep, but you got here. At this point your baby has learned, largely from you, how to soothe herself, saving you the need to intervene to help her. As we described in Chapter 5, by this point in her life your baby has acquired a fair number of "tools" and abilities to help calm and soothe herself.

Look, Ma!

By six months, you have a pretty good working knowledge of normal infant development. You could probably correctly answer the pediatrics medical board exam questions dealing with development during the first six months. One of the dirty little secrets of pediatrics is that an experienced parent knows as much pediatrics as many pediatric interns in training! When I took my pediatric boards and I got to a question about infant development, I didn't recall my medical training. I simply asked myself, "What were my own boys doing at that age?"

Dr. Mom

And speaking of the parent as pediatrician, by six months of life you have a wealth of experience in how to take care of a baby who isn't feeling well. Even if you were one of the lucky parents whose baby never had a fever during the first six months, you have learned by osmosis how to read the difference between a baby who feels well and one who doesn't. Most importantly, you have gained so much knowledge about your baby that you are better equipped than even your pediatrician at handling most minor illnesses of infancy. I mean that seriously: You are not *as good* as your pediatrician at caring for minor illnesses; you are *better* at it!

But if you have any doubts as to whether your baby needs more attention than Dr. Mom can provide, you are probably right. Your instinct can inform you when something falls out of the range of normal for your baby. At this point, your pediatrician would be happy to help you sort out what's going on with your baby.

From the standpoint of both your baby's health and the public health, by six months your baby has received the primary, or initial, series of vaccines against some formerly dangerous diseases of childhood. After her first shots at two months she may have been fussy and feverish, but by the six-month shots, I find that the reactions are much milder.

Your Baby's Changing Relationship to Medicine

The six-month mark is a huge milestone not only in terms of your baby's growth and development but also in terms of her relationship to the world of pediatrics. Here's why.

The meaning of "fever" changes

The meaning of "fever" changes because of the vaccines that we've already given your baby. At six months of age, your baby completes her primary series of three vaccines against a few previously dangerous diseases of childhood. Because of these vaccines (primarily the Hib and pneumococcal vaccines), the risk of serious bacterial infections such as meningitis and pneumonia drops substantially. The risk drops so low that the relationship between body temperature (fever) and your baby changes dramatically.

At six months, a fully immunized baby's temperature becomes a very unreliable measure of how sick she is, so the thermometer becomes a distraction. The number on the thermometer no longer gives you reliable information about how sick your child is. The thermometer distracts you from what is truly important—that is, the appearance of the baby in front of you. Can she look you in the eyes? Can she smile? Does she play at all? Can she drink fluids? (This last question is very important.)

At six months, in the case of a fully immunized baby, the most accurate devices in your house to assess how sick your baby is are your *hands* and your *eyes*. If you feel your baby's skin and she feels hot (not just warm, but *hot*), or if you look at her and she's not smiling and appears ill to you, you should give her comfort medication (acetaminophen or ibuprofen) to help her feel better.

Knowing what the thermometer reads only does one thing in my experience: It triggers *panic*. And panic is never a good thing, especially when taking care of a sick baby. Trust your hands and your eyes: They are far more reliable than the thermometer for a fully immunized, six-month-old baby.

So what should you do with that thermometer at the six-month point? I ask parents what they would do if they were tempted to take the baby's temperature. For parents able to resist the temptation, I recommend that they hide the thermometer in case they might use it for a subsequent baby. If, on the other hand, either or both parents don't believe they could resist the temptation and would take out the thermometer, I recommend the following: *Throw it away*!

Your baby has broadened her repertoire

One of the reasons you can dispose of the thermometer at six months is that the baby has a much broader repertoire of facial expressions and gestures that can tell you what's going on with her. For example, if her gums are bothering her, she can purposely place one or both hands in her mouth (or try to put anything else she can get in her mouth). She can show calm, worry, happiness, displeasure, and a host of other expressions. The baby's broader "vocabulary" helps parents enormously to understand the cues the baby sends.

A Tip from Dr Rob:

Signs That Your Baby May Be Sicker

- She won't smile anymore.
- She refuses to nurse or drink, no matter how persuasive you are.
- She won't play or interact with you.
- She won't make eye contact with you.

By six months, your baby will have expanded her repertoire of expressions. Her eyesight will be as good as yours, and her eye contact will be riveting.

Your baby graduates to the only effective teething remedy

One other huge milestone at six months is your baby's ability to take the only effective medication for the pain and discomfort of teething, and that is ibuprofen (Motrin/Advil). At less than six months of age, we don't recommend ibuprofen because it tends to be too harsh on a young infant's stomach.

The pain and discomfort of teething is too deep below the surface of the gum for a topical anesthetic to have any effect. Only ibuprofen, which is an anti-inflammatory, seems to dull the pain. Ibuprofen is also a good fever reducer, but it is much more effective at reducing inflammation than acetaminophen (Tylenol).

Many parents ask me if they can give ibuprofen every day for teething. The answer is that if you are giving the medication in doses appropriate for the baby's weight and if you are giving it only once per day (generally at night), you can give ibuprofen every day for several days in a row. If you give the medication only if the baby is having a bad night with teething, there is very little chance you will give too much ibuprofen.

Other Milestones

At the six-month stage, your baby's eating and sleeping patterns change and she becomes both more physically adept and surprisingly mobile. It's a whole new world for her—and for you!

Mmmmmm... Food! The first solids

At six months, most babies begin to eat solid foods. Feeding the baby solids for the first time is always a special and meaningful experience for new parents. We won't go into the details of feeding solids here: It's beyond the scope of this book. There are many excellent resources and websites with advice on how to introduce solids. I'll make only a few general observations. First, I have a bias toward real food as opposed to prepared baby food. The latter is packed with preservatives and artificial ingredients. Real vegetables and fruits, on the other hand, are better for the baby's health, they taste better, and they are far cheaper than jarred baby food.

Night-night! A new regimen

Once babies start eating solid foods at six months, the whole sleeping picture changes. If a baby eats two or three times during the day on top of the nursing and/or formula

A Tip from Dr Rob:

Making and Storing Your Own Baby Food

If you know how to use a blender or food processor, you already know how to make baby food! One trick we used to make a blender-full, for instance, of sweet potatoes last a while was to pour the contents of the blender into an ice tray and freeze the cubes so that we could take out individual servings whenever we wanted.

that she's taking, she should be consuming enough calories that she won't need to wake up during the night to feed. Babies who, at six months, are still feeding in the middle of the night are probably doing so more out of habit than hunger. This is the time when parents can work to get the baby to skip that 2:00 a.m. feeding and fall back to sleep. And, if you haven't removed the binkie, six months is best time to do so—right before the window of opportunity slams shut.

New tricks

After six months, your baby will be able to do all kinds of things that she couldn't do in the first half of her first year. Her head control will be so good that she can keep her relatively large head upright at will for extended periods. She may be able to sit up alone, or at least with someone or something supporting her hips. She may be much better at supporting herself on her legs when you hold her up. Most babies love this position and will stay there as long as you hold them or until they get hungry.

Is Bouncy Baby Bad?

A Tip from Dr Rob:

There's an unfortunate myth out there that the standing position is bad for babies and that it causes bowlegs. This is not true. Babies are naturally bow-legged. No amount of holding the baby upright and letting her bounce is going to make her more bow-legged than she already is. In fact, I call the bouncing baby a "win-win-win" situation: The baby enjoys it; parents love watching their babies enjoying themselves; and it's a developmental milestone that I check off my list.

Safety first

After six months, most babies have figured out some way to move from one place to another, even if only by wiggling. That's why I counsel parents never to leave their six-month-old alone unrestrained on any surface that is higher than the floor and turn their backs. Babies can move quickly.

Final Thoughts

My hope is that by the six-month mark you've come to understand that your baby is blessed to have been born here and now. Statistically speaking, your baby is among the healthiest human beings who have ever lived. I hope you've come to appreciate that your baby is an essentially healthy person. To repeat, that means it is a feature of your child's essence that she is healthy. Things may happen to her along the way: She may catch a stomach bug, she may bonk her head, but she'll remain essentially healthy.

One of the great joys of being a pediatrician is the knowledge that even the sickest children in my practice are likely to recover, fully, from whatever life sends their way. This is another feature of a baby's essence: a wonderful, nearly magical capacity to heal. I often joke with parents that if one is going to be sick or require surgery, it is best to be a child. Children recover from illness, injury, and surgery much more quickly and much more completely than adults do.

If more parents understood and believed that their babies were essentially healthy humans, a few important consequences would follow.

There would be far fewer visits to the pediatrician. Parents who are armed with knowledge born of experience and the confidence of their convictions can take care of the overwhelming majority of things that happen to their babies. Confident, knowledgeable parents appreciate that the range of normal is broad. That is to say, the rates at which children develop new skills and abilities vary widely. If your baby isn't rolling over or sitting up at the same age as your niece or nephew, or if she isn't gaining weight as quickly (or if she's gaining weight much more quickly), it does not mean that there is something wrong with your baby. There are plenty of opportunities for your pediatrician to take a look at your baby during her first year of life. There is little chance that something important will be missed or will fall through the cracks. Trust yourself: You will not miss something big and important!

Fewer visits to the doctor means that fewer prescriptions for antibiotics would be written. Many parents ask me how many ear infections my boys have had. The honest answer is that I don't know. The reason I don't know is that I have never looked in my boys' ears, and we almost never took either boy to their pediatrician. The surest way to obtain a diagnosis of an ear infection is to have a physician look in a child's ears (this probability doubles if that physician is an emergency department physician!). If parents understood that 80% of true bacterial ear infections resolve without antibiotics, we might start to reverse the epidemic of antibiotic-resistant germs that plagues our communities today.

There would be fewer pediatricians! In a world where parents understand and feel confident managing minor illnesses and understand the implications of the broad range of normal growth and development, there would be much less need for the services of a trained medical expert in diseases of childhood. In such a world, pediatricians would likely retreat to the hospitals for sick children from whence we emerged over one hundred years ago and care for the children who so desperately need our services. And we would begin to see a dwindling number of

Training in the Wrong Direction

I was trained in general pediatrics to care for children who are sick. Though well-child care was part of our training, the bulk of the teaching was directed at caring for children with problems, not with the overwhelming majority of children who are well and don't need to see a doctor. As a result, when I was graduated from residency, I was trained to view all children, even the well ones, through the prism of illness. That would have served me well had I remained in hospital work seeing sick children. Out in the community of well children, however, this type of pediatric training leads my colleagues and me to see abnormalities where none exist and to worry parents needlessly as a result.

board-certified pediatric specialists in the community providing routine care such as well visits and vaccinations. This is probably as it should be.

Nurse practitioners, physician assistants, and family practitioners would take on the primary care of healthy babies. Very likely, if pediatricians returned to the job of caring for the sickest children, the task of doing primary care (well visits, sick visits) would be transferred into the hands of an emerging group of professionals who are extremely well-suited for the job: nurse practitioners (NPs) and physician assistants (PAs). And we may see more children under the care of family practitioners (FPs, formerly known as general practitioners, or GPs). Many a day in the course of my practice I wish I were able to treat the child's parents as well, because so many of the problems I deal with are family problems rather than individual childhood problems. I'm speaking about lifestyle issues such as diet choices and exercise. It does little good to a child to recommend that he moderate his diet and increase exercise if I cannot manage his mother's high blood pressure and obesity as well! Family practitioners are best suited to help guide entire families to healthy lifestyle choices.

Parents would increasingly turn to the emerging valuable resource of the Internet. If books such as these cannot replace many of the functions of the pediatrician, surely the Internet can. In my view, the Internet is unfairly tagged as being a dangerous place to go for medical information. To the contrary: The Internet is a good place to get medical information. There is a lot of junk information on the web, but there's also a lot of bad advice and information you can get in doctors' offices. I recommend that you research any and all advice that you receive from a doctor. In "Recommended Web Resources" at the end of this book, I list some reliable and useful Internet-based resources that provide up-to-date and reliable information that can help you answer your medical questions and interpret the advice you are getting. The Internet can help you ask better questions of your physician as well.

I hope this book has empowered you with the tools to bolster your already growing base of knowledge and confidence as you raise your children. It's a well-worn path that you've embarked upon. Happy travels!

Skin Deep

Human skin is an organ that, at birth, has to make huge adjustments to living in a different medium and being exposed to different stimuli than it encountered in the womb. So it's no wonder that odd, scary-looking things crop up on baby skin from time to time. Lots of things can and will appear on your baby's skin. All of them look terrible. All of them have truly nasty-sounding Latinate names. And all of them are completely benign and go away without any treatment whatsoever.

First Days

Get ready for white and blue spots on your newborn.

Erythema toxicum: In the first few days of life, it's typical for a rash that looks like mosquito bites to appear at random sites around your baby's body, hang around for a day or so, then disappear only to reappear elsewhere. These are not actual mosquito bites. Most likely there are no mosquitoes in your hospital room. The name notwithstanding, Erythema toxicum, or ET, is neither toxic nor red and has nothing to do with extraterrestrials. It is a normal baby rash that has no known cause and disappears as suddenly and as inexplicably as it appears.

Milia: Often your baby will develop tiny white spots on her nose and possibly surrounding areas. Milia is another completely benign rash that takes longer to disappear but will go away just as surely as ET. Please resist the temptation to squeeze these spots. They are not pimples.

Blue Spots: Some babies are born with patches on their buttocks, backs, and other areas that resemble bruises. They are not bruises; they are Blue Spots. Blue Spots are common in people who come from regions of the world where skin tones are darker, particularly Asia, which is why the patches developed their old, less politically correct name: Mongolian Spots. Sadly, since some caregivers don't know what Blue Spots are, they may accuse parents of abuse. If your baby has Blue Spots, it's best to show them to caregivers and explain what they are *before* they ask.

Narrow tear ducts: Many babies have one or two teary or goopy eyes. Rather than an indication of conjunctivitis, it's probably caused by a narrow or blocked tear duct. Everything on a newborn is small, but the tiny holes at the inside (nose-side) corner of each eye are particularly small and clog easily. When they get clogged, the baby's natural tears have nowhere to go, so it appears that the baby is crying when she isn't. The other natural products that eyes produce also build up and appear to be goopy, but it's not an infection and doesn't require drops or medication.

If your baby has narrow or blocked tear ducts, simply wipe the goop away with a warm terrycloth towel. Then massage beneath the eye: Start at the nose and move down and out toward the corner of baby's mouth. It's best to do this while the baby is feeding. If you touch a baby's face when she's not feeding, you'll trigger her rooting reflex and she'll start to look for a nipple. That's not nice to do to a baby unless you actually plan to feed her!

First Month(s)

Just when you thought all the weird rashes from the newborn nursery were gone for good, new ones appear. Just like those rashes from the first couple days, these rashes also have terrible-sounding Latin names and they're pretty nasty looking. Best of all, you usually don't have to put anything on them and they go away without treatment.

Zits: At around one month of age, spots begin to appear on the baby's cheeks. They look an awful lot like pimples. In fact, they *are* pimples. This is *Acne neonatorum*, or baby acne. It tends to spread and get worse before it gets better. Baby acne can cover the entire head, may spread on the chest as far as the nipple-line, and sometimes spreads a similar distance down the back. It tends to go away completely by six weeks of age, but sometimes can last into the first several months of life.

Baby acne occurs for some of the same reasons that pregnant mothers get acne: pregnancy hormones. Remember that the baby had been swimming in pregnant-woman hormones for almost ten months. Now that she's out in the world, she isn't exposed to the source of those hormones (mom) any longer, and she begins to break them down, pee them out, and otherwise get rid of them. It is this hormone withdrawal that causes baby acne.

Our first baby had terrible baby acne. I remember standing over the bassinet with my wife gazing down at our four-week-old boy. And I remember shaking my head and clucking my tongue and saying, "Oh my God! We can't take him outside. He's too frightening-looking." But, of course, within a few days the zits were gone and he went back to being his cute self.

Those embarrassing flakes: Even more common than baby acne is *Seborrheic derma-titis*, or more commonly, *cradle cap*. This is the name given to the dry white or yellow flakes that can appear anywhere where there's hair on the infant's head (including her eyebrows) but is much more common on the top in the center, just over the baby's *fontanelle* (soft spot). We call these flakes cradle cap or Seborrheic dermatitis because we don't like to call it by its even more common name, dandruff. Rarely, a fungus that also causes diaper rash produces the white or yellow flakes, but most often the flakes have no cause. Like baby acne, for most babies cradle cap goes away on its own, but for some children, particularly those whose cradle cap is complicated by fungal skin rashes, the condition can last longer.

I don't like to treat cradle cap. For one thing, true cradle cap doesn't bother the infant. In fact, it bothers us far more to look at it than it bothers the baby. If the baby wiggles her head a lot, trying to scratch it as though it itches, the rash might be something other than cradle cap, like eczema (see below). Another reason not to treat cradle cap is that the treatment is often worse than the skin condition. Shampoos that contain selenium or tar are difficult to use because they sting terribly if you get them in your baby's eyes.

It turns out that baby oil and a fine-tooth comb can be a good, non-medical way to get rid of cradle cap, if only temporarily. Most parents, especially parents with more than one child, don't have the time to bother with a benign condition that doesn't bother the child.

I once knew a first-time mom who had access to some high-quality, extra-virgin olive oil and some high-end oil of camphor she had acquired from her native India. She placed a single drop of the oil of camphor in a cup of the olive oil and painstakingly combed the mixture through her newborn baby boy's hair. She brought him in the next day to show me. She did an absolutely *spectacular* job! This little one-month old had movie-star-quality hair—very beautiful and very unnecessary. But I complimented her on her excellent work. Needless to say when she had subsequent children, she did not work so hard to treat their cradle cap.

Elbows, knees, and ears—baby eczema: In the first several weeks of life, *Infantile eczema*, or *Atopic dermatitis*, can appear anywhere on a baby's body, but there are a few classic locations. The most common spot is behind the ear near the earlobe. It's also common to see it in the folds of the elbows and the knees. It tends to look red or brown and scaly. Sometimes it can look greasy and may weep little bits of fluid. Sometimes breaks in the skin can occur with small amounts of bleeding.

About half the time we have no idea why babies get eczema. For the rest of the cases, especially if the eczema is severe or covers a large area of the baby's body, the reason could be a food allergy. If your baby has eczema, especially bad eczema, this is a topic you can bring up with your pediatrician. I discuss food allergies at more length in Chapter 4. The good news is that these food allergies are not necessarily lifelong, and you can eliminate them by diet.

One way you can minimize the baby's eczema is to slather her with lots of greasy emollients like petroleum jelly or the fancier name-brand products. The baby may end up looking a little greasy, but she doesn't care what she looks like—she's much more interested in having comfortable skin than in looking pretty.

Another way to avoid making eczema worse is to limit baths. When you do bathe your baby, use tepid—never hot—water since this really irritates sensitive skin. For moderate to severe eczema, you may use a low-potency, over-the-counter steroid cream, 1% hydrocortisone, three times per day. If you're putting hydrocortisone on your baby's face, do so only for a week, since facial skin tends to be sensitive to steroids. If the skin is broken, apply an over-the-counter topical antibiotic as you would to keep cuts from getting infected.

Birthmarks: The term *birthmark* is a misnomer. One of the distinguishing features of birthmarks is that they are rarely present at birth. More often, birthmarks appear in the first few days to the first few weeks of life. There are many different types and subtypes of birthmarks that could appear on your baby's skin. For the purposes of this chapter it's useful to talk about spots in two groups, *pigmented* and *vascular* (composed of blood vessels).

Brown, blue, and cafe-au-lait: Brown spots, or *nevi* (the singular is *nevus*), can appear anywhere on the body. They tend to be smaller than the head of a pencil-eraser and they tend to be a nice uniform color. Sometimes, however, they can be larger and show many different shades of brown. The overwhelming majority of these birthmarks are absolutely normal, so there isn't anything you need to do about them until well into adulthood, if not old age. If you think a baby's brown spot is changing, the best thing you can do is take a picture of it with an object of known size, like a coin. If the spot continues to change or grow, you can take a comparison photograph. Dermatologists *love* photographs. Comparison photographs are an invaluable resource for your pediatrician and for a dermatologist if a referral should become necessary. Referrals, however, are rarely needed.

The vascular birthmarks: Port-wine marks usually occur in the middle of the baby's forehead but can also appear on the eyelids, the nose, or even the lips. Sometimes these marks look like tongues of flame, so they have been called *flame nevi*, or in Latin, *Nevus flammeus.* The neat thing about flame nevi is that they get darker when the baby cries. This is because these marks are made of microscopic blood vessels (capillaries). They are completely benign and usually go away over the first several months of life.

The other common location for these port-wine stains is the nape of the neck. These marks are affectionately referred to as "stork-bites," as in the little white lie we tell children about where babies come from. Whereas modern depictions of the stork illustrate the bird carrying the baby in a cloth sling, earlier versions apparently depicted the bird grabbing the baby directly by the back of the neck.

Parents always ask me if the mark is going to go away. I used to answer their question with another question: "You've seen lots of babies who have these flame marks, but have you ever seen an adult who has one?" One day a new mom in my practice asked me if her baby's flame would go away. I asked my usual question and she responded,

"Well, *mine* didn't go away!" It turns out she wore makeup to cover a small port-wine stain. This mom is so far the *only* adult I've ever seen with a flame nevus on her forehead, but I no longer answer new parents' questions with another question.

Sometimes port-wine stains can be deeper in color and more pronounced than the common flame nevus. These often don't go away. This is another topic you can discuss with your pediatrician.

There's a special category of vascular birthmarks: the *strawberry* or *hemangioma*. Hemangiomata are actually benign growths of blood vessels. They appear in the first few weeks of life and grow throughout the first year. At one year (though sometimes earlier), hemangiomata begin to soften and disappear. Half of all hemangiomata are completely gone by age five. Ninety percent are gone by age nine.

Infant Vaccination Schedule

Age	Hep B	DTaP	Hib	PCV-13	IPV	Rota
Birth	X					
2 months		X	X	X	X	X
4 months	X	X	X	X	X	X
6 months	X	X	X	X	X	X

See Chapter 9 for a more in-depth look at these vaccines.

Hep B (Hepatitis B): Your baby can take the first hepatitis B vaccine in the hospital before going home, but as long as your ob-gyn determines that you don't have hepatitis yourself, you can safely delay the vaccine until two months.

DTaP (Diphtheria, Tetanus, and acellular Pertussis): This vaccine can be given separately but is often given in combination with polio and Hib.

Hib (Hemophilus influenzae type B): This vaccine may also be given separately or in combination with other vaccines, as above.

PCV-13 (Pneumococcal): Often sold commercially as Prevnar, this vaccine protects against 13 types of the bacterium.

IPV (Intramuscular polio vaccine): This vaccine is named to distinguish it from the older oral polio vaccine (OPV).

Rota (Rotavirus vaccine): This is a live-attenuated oral vaccine. Unlike the other vaccines on this list, you must start giving it at two months of age or you lose the opportunity to give it at all!

Growth Charts

Pediatricians use these growth charts during well-baby office visits to chart infant growth over time. Please consult Chapter 7 for further information about infant growth.

Birth to 24 months: Boys
Length-for-age and Weight-for-age percentiles

NAME

RECORD #

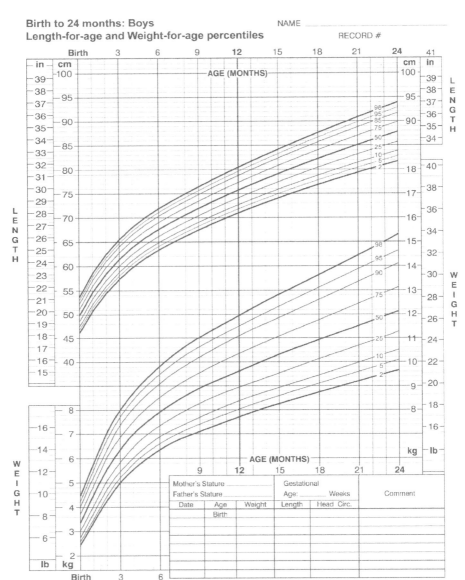

Published by the Centers for Disease Control and Prevention, November 1, 2009
SOURCE: WHO Child Growth Standards (http://www.who.int/childgrowth/en)

Birth to 24 months: Boys
Head circumference-for-age and
Weight-for-length percentiles

NAME

RECORD #

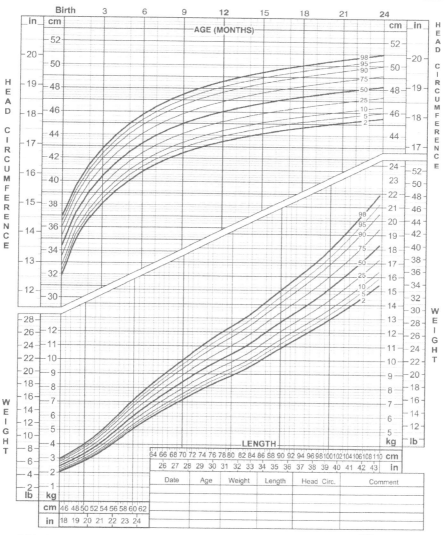

Published by the Centers for Disease Control and Prevention, November 1, 2009
SOURCE: WHO Child Growth Standards (http://www.who.int/childgrowth/en)

Birth to 24 months: Girls
Length-for-age and Weight-for-age percentiles

NAME _____

RECORD # _____

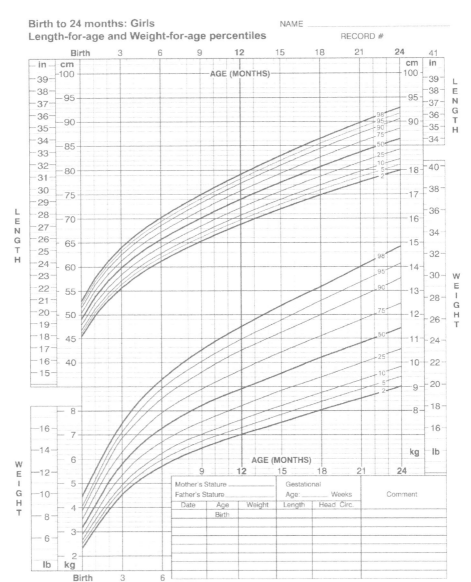

Published by the Centers for Disease Control and Prevention, November 1, 2009
SOURCE: WHO Child Growth Standards (http://www.who.int/childgrowth/en)

Birth to 24 months: Girls
Head circumference-for-age and
Weight-for-length percentiles

NAME _____

RECORD # _____

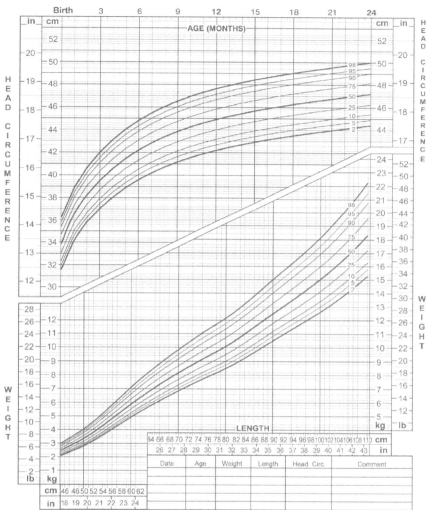

Published by the Centers for Disease Control and Prevention, November 1, 2009
SOURCE: WHO Child Growth Standards (http://www.who.int/childgrowth/en)

Well-Baby Visits

Well-baby office visits serve the following four purposes:

- To address any concerns you might have
- To perform a developmental assessment of your baby
- To prepare you for developmental changes that are likely to occur before the next well visit
- To immunize your baby against several formerly dangerous diseases of childhood

The first three items are covered at every visit (sometimes even at sick visits). With the exception of the first visit during the first week after discharge from the hospital, immunization schedules determine the timing and frequency of well visits.

The American Academy of Pediatrics recommends the order and timing of immunizations. Each provider changes the schedule only slightly for the sake of convenience but keeps all changes within guidelines set by the Academy.

Any Questions?

Before you arrive, it's always a good idea to write down any questions. These days, parents come to my office with questions prepared on one of the applications on their cell phones. Why write down questions? *Because chances are you won't ask those questions if you don't write them down.* I'm a physician, and even I forget to ask questions I had in mind to ask my doctor! Just in case you don't write down questions, many offices such as mine provide you with a form and a clipboard where you can write down things you want to discuss during the visit. In my office, this form includes questions that I want to document in the chart, such as the list of medications the baby may be taking and mentions of trips to an emergency department.

You should even write down the questions you are reluctant to ask. Often I glance over at the list a parent brings and notice that he or she skipped one of the questions, so I ask the parent about the neglected question. I figure if it was important enough to write down the parent probably wants to discuss it!

Then the doctor or practitioner may ask you a series of questions: about feeding, about behavior, about developmental milestones, and the like. While I ask these questions in my office, I watch the baby closely to see what she does and how she interacts with her parents and with me. I gain a lot of information this way without having to ask questions!

Remember that the office visit is not a performance. If you say that your baby can roll over we assume she can roll over! We don't expect a baby to perform for us in the office. If mom or dad says she can do something, she can do it!

The Once-Over

Then the baby gets her exam. This is usually brief, not least because babies are small and it's easy to see everything fairly quickly! Most doctors start at one end and move to the other. We look at the head, eyes, ears, nose, and mouth. Then we listen to the baby's chest for breathing and heart sounds. The belly is close so we will often listen there as well.

Very often the doctor holds the baby's knees and presses down and out to test for stability of the hips. Even if the baby's hips were stable at each previous exam, we still check. It doesn't bother the baby and it helps us keep our checklist of exam items intact. Then we finish with a quick survey of the baby's reflexes and sensations and we're done.

What's Next?

This is the point in the visit where we often talk about the next couple months: what new skills the baby may acquire, what changes to expect, and so on. It's also an opportunity for you to ask more questions.

Shots

The last part of the visit is always shots, the part the parents like the least. To tell the truth, it's my least favorite part of the visit as well, but I know that it's probably the most important part: preventing dangerous illnesses in your baby. I always remind parents that the baby may be fussier than usual, warmer than usual, or sleepier than usual after shots. If the baby is fussy or warm, I recommend acetaminophen (Tylenol) and we discuss the dose appropriate for the baby's weight.

A Tip from Dr Rob:

How to Make Shots as Painless as Humanly Possible

In my office, we give shots in the baby's thighs. I have the baby lie on her back and ask one of the parents to play with her hands. This is so that the baby doesn't try to grab at the syringe giving the shot! It also allows the parents to keep the baby's attention and talk or sing to her while we quickly give the injections. If there is more than one shot, I have a staff member give the first shot in one leg while I give the second shot in the other. This gets the procedure over more quickly. We quickly apply band-aids and have the parent pick up the baby immediately to comfort her.

On the way out, the front desk staff asks you to schedule the baby's next visit. You may also get a copy of the baby's growth charts (height, weight, and head circumference) as well as a record of immunizations if required by a childcare center.

Dr Rob's Recommended Web Resources for New Parents

Medscape: Easily searchable medical information on any topic
http://emedicine.medscape.com/

Kids Health: General information on parenting and baby health
http://kidshealth.org/parent/

UpToDate: As the name suggests, the most current medical information available on the web
http://www.uptodate.com/patients/index.html

The Food Allergy and Anaphylaxis Network: Information about babies with food allergies
http://www.foodallergy.org/

WebMD: Health and parenting
http://www.webmd.com/parenting/default.htm

Wikipedia: The much-maligned, unfairly criticized source for practically everything. Wikipedia forces the web searcher to examine the sources and decide for himself or herself whether the information is reliable. If there are no sources cited, Wikipedia alerts the reader that the information might not be good! You don't find that sort of thing in standard medical and parenting sites.
http://en.wikipedia.org/wiki/Main_Page

Index

S

safety
- at six months and beyond, 192
- vaccine-related controversies and, 177

scent, introducing newborn to your pet(s), 50

schedule
- infant vaccination, 203
- nudging baby toward, 115–116
- of parent-directed sleep methods, 104
- for twins/multiples, 116–117

scientific view of parent-baby bonding, 31–32

sclera, and conjunctivitis, 159–161

screening tests, 9–10

Sears, Dr. William, 110

Seborrheic dermatitis (cradle cap), 199

sedatives, as old-school colic therapy, 97

seizures, with fever, 145–146

self-soothing
- child development and, 105
- Ferber sleep method for babies after, 109
- transition to, 95

Semmelweis, Ignaz, 5

sensory stimulation
- babies preferring low-sensory environment, 23–24
- removing for easily distracted babies, 82–83

A Shot in the Dark (book), 174

shushing sound, for colic, 99

sibling(s)
- introducing newborn to its, 49
- not nursing simultaneously, 75
- sleep-training in presence of, 114

sick visits, to doctor, 165

side/stomach position, colic, 98

SIDS (Sudden Infant Death Syndrome), 106–107, 111

singing to baby, 34

six months and beyond
- broadened repertoire of expressions, 190–191
- feeding, 186–187
- knowledge of infant development, 187
- meaning of fever at, 189–190
- other milestones, 192–193
- signs your baby may be sicker, 190
- sleeping, 187
- soothing, 187
- taking care of sick baby, 187–188
- teething remedy for, 191–192
- you are an expert by now, 186

skin
- antibiotic ointment for breaks in, 162
- baby crying to be next to your, 88
- baby eczema on, 200
- birthmarks on, 200–202
- brown spots on, 201
- cold baby showing mottled, 16
- cradle cap, 199–200
- early follow-up for jaundice, 8–9
- first days, 197–198
- first months, 198–199
- hair tourniquet pinching, 91
- less bathing to preserve oils in, 17–18
- losing elasticity when dehydrated, 143
- moisturizing baby's peeling, 18
- not using rubbing alcohol on, 148
- rashes. *see* rashes
- signs of illness, 142

sleep associations
- eliminating adverse, 108–109, 112
- three temptations to avoid when breaking, 113–114
- troubleshooting, 112–113

sleeping
- associations with, 112–114
- baby-directed methods of, 106–110
- defining normal, 103
- eat-well, sleep-well formula, 103
- getting babies to, 103–104
- go-to-sleep philosophy of Dr. Rob, 112
- happens, 101–102
- napping and nighttime, 117–119
- parent-directed methods of, 105–106
- popular methods for, 104–105
- risks of bed sharing, 111
- schedules and, 115–116
- siblings and, 114
- at six months and beyond, 186–187, 192–193
- in strange places, 118–119
- troubleshooting, 119–120
- twins/multiples and, 116–117
- for whole family, 114–115

slow grower, evaluating, 129–130

smallpox
- eradication of, 171–172
- Jenner introduces inoculation, 171
- legal precedent of vaccination for, 179
- as severe risk in eighteenth century, 178
- and variolation procedure, 170–171

smiling
- overview of, 29
- as reliable indicator of illness, 142

social smile
- gas smile or, 39

More great books from the *What Now?* Series!

Lesson Ladder is dedicated to helping you prepare for life's most fundamental challenges. We provide practical tools and well-rounded advice that help you achieve your goals while climbing the personal or professional ladder—whether it is preparing to start a family of your own, getting your child potty trained, or learning a new kind of financial management.

I'm Having a Baby! Well-Rounded Perspectives
Collective wisdom for a more comforting and "balanced" understanding of what to expect during pregnancy, childbirth, and the days that follow. $16.99

Making Kid Time Count for Ages 0–3: The Attentive Parent Advantage
Whether you're a working or stay-at-home parent, this book shows you how to maximize your time with your baby or toddler, with tips for developing a strong parent-child relationship and ways to ensure strong cognitive, social, and emotional development for your child. $16.99

I'm Potty Training My Child: Proven Methods That Work
Respecting that children and parenting styles differ, we created this guide to offer a variety of effective training solutions to help today's busy parents with easy, fast reading, and even faster results! $12.99

Better Behavior for Ages 2–10: Small Miracles That Work Like Magic
For the harried parent, this book offers the compassion, help, and proven solutions you need to manage—and prevent—difficult child behavior. $16.99

Call toll-free to order! **1-800-301-4647**
Or order online: **www.LessonLadder.com**

CPSIA information can be obtained at www.ICGtesting.com
Printed in the USA
LVOW01s2036250913

354110LV00018B/27/P